New

▓k-free, Egg-free

▓es for Children

New
Milk-free, Egg-free
Recipes for Children

by Pauline Moore

Nutritional Therapy for allergenic symptoms including eczema, asthma, diarrhoea, colic, coeliac disease and ulcerative colitis

W. FOULSHAM & CO. LTD
LONDON · NEW YORK · TORONTO
CAPE TOWN · SYDNEY

*To my husband Barry and children,
Caroline, Giles and Mark with love.*

Cover photograph courtesy of Johnson & Johnson

W. FOULSHAM & COMPANY LIMITED
Yeovil Road, SLOUGH, Berkshire, SL1 4JH,
ENGLAND

ISBN 0-572-01401-5

I should like to thank Mrs Sheila Milner for her
boundless patience and accurate typing; Patricia
Robertson for all her help and encouragement;
Mrs Wendy Hobson for her sympathetic
handling of the text; and the many
manufacturers, dieticians, authors, publishers
and others who so generously supplied me
with information and answered my questions.

Printed in Great Britain by St. Edmundsbury Press,
Bury St. Edmunds, Suffolk.

CONTENTS

INTRODUCTION

As early as 1901 a German, F. Hamburger, foresaw the possibility of an allergic reaction to cow's milk protein. Since that first report there have been numerous medical articles published confirming that cow's milk allergy and egg allergy are two very common allergies indeed.

In fact, many eminent doctors now recommend that if there is a family history of asthma, coeliac disease, eczema, lactose intolerance or allergy or food intolerance of any kind, the development of these symptoms could possibly be prevented if cow's milk is withheld until infants are six months old, and eggs until they are one year old.

Food allergy is no fun for the sensitive individual. A small amount of the allergen can bring on symptoms, whether mild or severe, within a few minutes.

The ideal way of dealing with food allergy is to eliminate the offending food from the diet. In some cases this is easy, but in other cases, where the allergen may be an ingredient in other foods and drinks, it is more difficult. This is the case with milk and eggs.

If one looks in any cookery book one will find on almost every page recipes that demand milk or eggs. My intention was to write a cookery book totally without milk and eggs, which caters specifically for children, while at the same time trying to keep their diet as normal as possible in all respects, and to ensure good nutrition and growth.

Every recipe in this book is therefore, completely milk-free, egg-free and lactose free.

NOTES ON THE RECIPES

All the recipes serve four people except those in the BABY FOOD section, which serve one.

Cup and spoon measures are level.

Do not mix metric, Imperial and American measures; follow one set only.

SHOPPING HINTS

Milk and eggs seem to find their way into the most unexpected food products. Indeed, their versatility is sometimes amazing.

It is therefore important when shopping for food products to look very closely at the list of ingredients, which is usually printed on the packet, jar or can, to make quite sure that milk or eggs have not been added.

They can be described in the following ways: **albumen, butter, buttermilk, casein, cheese, cheese powder, chocolate, cream, dried egg, dried whey, egg protein, egg white solids, lactose, low-fat milk, margarine, milk fat, milk protein, separated milk solids, skimmed milk, sodium caseinate, whey, whole milk, yoghurt**.

Do remember that one product, for example, toast spread, may be milk- or egg-free in one brand and may not be in another – if you are in any doubt, don't buy.

FOODS TO AVOID

The following list shows a range of products which usually contain milk or eggs. It is not possible to give a more comprehensive list because manufacturers frequently alter their ingredients. If approached, however, most manufacturers are usually extremely obliging in supplying a list of their current milk- and egg-free products.
Batter mixes.
Biscuits.
Butter.

Cakes and cake mixes.

Casilan powder.

Cheese, cheese spreads and processed cheese.

Chocolate and cocoa products, including chocolate drinks. The British Dietetic Association have advised some manufacturers that both cocoa material and also coconut products are unsuitable for those suffering from galactosaemia.

Coffeemate, Coffee complement etc.

Cream.

Custard and quick custard.

Dessert toppings.

Egg, egg white.

Fudge.

Ice-cream and ice-cream products.

Lemon curd and lemon cheese.

Malted drinks such as Bournvita, Horlicks, Ovaltine and Chocolate Ovaltine.

Margarine, polyunsaturated, soft or hard margarine with the exception of Tomor or recommended milk-free margarine (see page 11).

Mayonnaise and canned foods with added mayonnaise.

Milk in all forms, e.g. fresh, evaporated, condensed, dried or skimmed.

Pies.

Puddings and cream puddings.

Toffee.

Virol.

Yoghurt.

PROPRIETARY FOODS WHICH MAY CONTAIN MILK OR EGGS

As brands vary, some of these types of foods will contain milk or eggs, so it is wise to check the label when buying.

Baby foods.

Baking powder. Commercial makes may contain lactose, added to improve the keeping quality of the powder. To make home-made baking powder, use one part sodium bicarbonate to two parts cream of tartar. Store in an airtight container.

Bread.

Breakfast cereals.

Fish products coated with batter or crumbs, fish pastes, spreads and pâtés.

Instant mashed potato.

Meat products coated with batter and crumbs, meat pies and pasties, pastes, spreads and pâtés (including toast spreads). Some canned and packet meat products. Sausages and sausage rolls.

Pasta and some prepared pasta foods. Egg-free pastas are available.

Soups and sauces, both canned and packet, and canned or frozen foods in sauce.

Wine is frequently cleared with egg white.

FOODS TO LOOK FOR

At the back of the book, you will find recipes for milk-free milk, pastry and butters which are used in many of the recipes. In addition, the following products are extremely useful.

Baby rice. Robinson's baby rice is milk-free and lactose-free.

Carob. For those intolerant to chocolate, try using carob instead. There are recipes for Carob coating and Carob icing on page 156. Some proprietary carob products may contain milk.

Milk-free margarine. Tomor margarine is specially prepared for the Jewish household. It contains no milk products and is therefore ideal for milk-free, lactose-free diets. Tomor may be found in branches of most large supermarket chains and health food shops. If, however, you have difficulty finding Tomor, contact the manufacturers:

Van den Berghs & Jurgens Ltd., Sussex House, Burgess Hill, West Sussex, RH15 9AW.

Outside Britain, the address for stockists information is:

International Distributors, GIB Ltd., 31 Withams Road, PO Box 70, Gibraltar.

Polyunsaturated milk free margarine. 'Vitaquell Extra' is a low cholesterol, polyunsaturated, non-hydrogenated, low sodium, milk-free margarine. It is guaranteed by the manufacturer to be free of milk, milk extracts, animal protein and lactose. 'Vitaquell Extra' may be used for spreading or in many of the recipes in this book by those on low cholesterol, high polyunsaturated diets.

Low sodium, milk-free margarine. 'Vitasieg' is an unsalted, low sodium, soft, milk-free margarine, which may be used for frying, baking and table use. 'Vitasieg' and 'Vitaquell Extra' are both available from health food shops.

Milk-free margarine. The following brands of milk-free margarine have been recommended for use in the countries mentioned below, and may be used in the recipes in this book instead of Tomor.

Australia. 'Nuttlex', 'Sundew', 'Becel'.

Canada. 'Fleischmann's' unsalted, low sodium, 100% corn oil.

South Africa. All 'Yellow' margarine is milk-free, for example, 'Floro', 'Rama', 'Sunshine D', 'Stork'.

USA. 'Diet Mazola', 'Mazola Margarine', 'Imperial Diet Margarine', 'Mother's Brand Margarine', 'Willow Run Soybean Margarine', 'Parkay Diet Margarine'.

Do not substitute Tomor or another milk-free margarine with other brands of margarine unless you know them to be milk-free. If in doubt, always check with your doctor or dietician first.

Terry's Bitter Bar. Terry's Bitter Bar contains no milk products. It is suitable for milk-free, lactose-free diets. Do not substitute in recipes with plain chocolate, which may contain butterfat, added to improve its keeping properties.

Vitamins. To maintain good health and prevent deficiency, a lactose-free multivitamin and mineral supplement is recommended, including vitamin B_{12} for vegans.

MILK SUBSTITUTES

The following is a list of milk substitutes, one of which may be recommended by your child's doctor or dietician, and which may be available on prescription.

I have included the list in the book not only to supply you with further information, but also to reassure anxious parents that there is plenty of choice available.

Formula S Soya Food (Cow & Gate, UK). A powder prepared from soya protein isolate, glucose syrup, and vegetable oil, with added vitamins and minerals.
Use: to replace milk for those suffering from lactose intolerance and milk protein intolerance.

Galactomin Formula 17 (Cow & Gate, UK). A powder containing in each 100g: fat 22.3g, protein 22.3g, carbohydrates 50.2g, and mineral salts 3g. Requires vitamin supplementation.
Use: to replace milk in galactosaemia.

Galactomin Formula 18. As Galactomin 17, but with a reduced fat content.

Galactomin, Fructose Formula 19. As Galactomin 18, but with fructose.
Use: for glucose-galactose intolerance.

Nutramigen: (Bristol-Myers Pharmaceuticals, UK). Hydrolysed casein, sucrose, starch, and maize oil, with added vitamins and minerals; containing protein 15%, fat 18% and carbohydrate 59%.
Use: to replace milk in galactosaemia, milk protein intolerance and lactose intolerance.

Portagen: (Bristol-Myers Pharmaceuticals, UK). A complete food, supplied as powder for preparation with water before use. Contains: sodium caseinate, corn syrup solids, sucrose, and corn oil, with added vitamins and minerals; containing carbohydrate 54.3%, fat 22.5%, and protein 16.5%.
Use: lactose intolerance.

Pregestimil: (Bristol-Myers Pharmaceuticals, UK). Hydrolysed casein, amino acids, corn syrup solids, modified tapioca starch and maize oil, with added vitamins and minerals. It contains no lactose, gluten or sucrose.
Use: lactose intolerance and also suitable for "some" infants suffering from milk protein intolerance.

Prosobee Liquid: (Bristol-Myers Pharmaceuticals, UK). A concentrated liquid prepared from soya protein isolate, soya oil, corn syrup solids, and coconut oil, with added minerals and vitamins; containing protein 4%, fat 7.2% and carbohydrate 13.8%.
Use: to replace milk in galactosaemia, milk protein intolerance and lactose intolerance.

Prosobee Powder: A complete food prepared from similar ingredients to the above; containing protein 15.6%, fat 28%, and carbohydrate 51.6%. Gluten free.
Use: same as Liquid.

Velactin: (Wander, UK): A powdered milk substitute of vegetable origin, free from lactose and supplemented with vitamins and minerals; containing protein 12%, fat 19.5%, and carbohydrate 62%.

Use: lactose intolerance, milk protein intolerance, and as basic feed pending the identification of specific allergens.

Wysoy (Wyeth, UK): A powder prepared from soya protein isolate, corn syrup solids, sucrose, vegetable oils, destearinated fat, and coconut oil, with added vitamins and minerals; containing fat 48%, carbohydrate 39%, and protein 13%.
Use: to replace milk in galactosaemia, milk protein intolerance and lactose intolerance.

Wysoy Ready-to-Feed. As above, but in a ready-to-feed form.
Use: same as powder.

NOTES AND SUGGESTIONS

Baby clinic. Do take your baby to the clinic regularly. As well as allowing your baby's progress to be assessed, you can take the opportunity of talking over any problems you may have.

Doctor. Your family or clinic doctor should be the first person to consult if you suspect your child is suffering from an allergy or food intolerance.

Diet. Try to learn as much about food, and what it contains, as possible. The Food Composition Tables in the book are intended to be an introduction only. For a more comprehensive guide you will need *The Composition of Foods* (HMSO).

Egg replacer. I have not used an egg replacer in this book because its main constituent is 'Methycellulose'. Recent studies indicate that diets containing large amounts of Methycellulose might result in the decreased absorption of calcium and other minerals.

Health visitor. Confide in your health visitor. I found mine to be an invaluable help in the early months of my son's allergy.

Immunising injections. Certain immunising injections are prepared on an egg medium, such as those for influenza, measles and yellow fever. Parents of those children sensitive to eggs should inform the doctor or nurse of their child's allergy before their child receives any injection.

Kosher 'Pareve' products. Many large supermarkets now include a Kosher section in which you may find many useful milk-free products to expand your child's diet.

Re-introducing foods. Try re-introducing the foods to which your child is intolerant in very small quantities after an interval of three to six months. If a food causes a severe reaction, it should not be eaten again unless your child's doctor or dietician specifically recommend the re-introduction of the offending allergen.

Visiting. Always make sure your friends and relatives know about your child's allergy, so that they do not inadvertantly give them some food to which they are intolerant.

RECOMMENDED DAILY AMOUNTS OF FOOD ENERGY AND SOME NUTRIENTS

(from DHSS 1979)

Age range (a) years	Energy		Protein	Thiamin	Riboflavin	Nicotinic acid equivalents mg	Ascorbic acid	Vitamin A retinol equivalents	Vitamin D(b) cholecalciferol	Calcium	Iron
	MJ	Kcal	g	mg	mg		mg	µg	µg	mg	mg
BOYS											
1	5.0	1200	30	0.5	0.6	7	20	300	10	600	7
2	5.75	1400	35	0.6	0.7	8	20	300	10	600	7
3-4	6.5	1560	39	0.6	0.8	9	20	300	10	600	8
5-6	7.25	1740	43	0.7	0.9	10	20	300	(b)	600	10
7-8	8.25	1980	49	0.8	1.0	11	20	400	(b)	600	10
9-11	9.5	2280	57	0.9	1.2	14	25	575	(b)	700	12
12-14	11.0	2640	66	1.1	1.4	16	25	725	(b)	700	12
15-17	12.0	2880	72	1.2	1.7	19	30	750	(b)	600	12

| Age range (a) years | Energy | | Protein | Thiamin | Riboflavin | Nicotinic acid equiv- | Ascorbic acid | Vitamin A retinol equiv- | Vitamin D(b) chole- | Calcium | Iron |
	MJ	Kcal	g	mg	mg	alents mg	mg	alents µg	calciferol µg	mg	mg
GIRLS											
1	4.5	1100	27	0.4	0.6	7	20	300	10	600	7
2	5.5	1300	32	0.5	0.7	8	20	300	10	600	7
3-4	6.25	1500	37	0.6	0.8	9	20	300	10	600	8
5-6	7.0	1680	42	0.7	0.9	10	20	300	(b)	600	10
7-8	8.0	1900	47	0.8	1.0	11	20	400	(b)	600	10
9-11	8.5	2050	51	0.8	1.2	14	25	575	(b)	700	12(c)
12-14	9.0	2150	53	0.9	1.4	16	25	725	(b)	700	12(c)
15-17	9.0	2150	53	0.9	1.7	19	30	750	(b)	600	12(c)

NOTES TO TABLE

(a) Since the recommendations are average amounts, the figure for each age range represents the amounts recommended at the middle of the range. Within each age range, younger children will need less, and older children more, than the amount recommended.

(b) No dietary sources may be necessary for children who are sufficiently exposed to sunlight, but during the winter children and adolescents should receive 10 µg (400 i.u.) daily by supplementation.

(c) This intake may not be sufficient for 10% of girls and women with large menstrual losses.

FOOD COMPOSITION TABLES

Food	Energy		protein	Fat	Carbo-hydrate	Vit B₁	Vit B₂	Nicotinic acid	Vit C	Vit A	Vit D	Calcium	Iron
	kcal	kj	g	G	g	mg	mg	mg	mg	μg	μg	mg	mg
							values per 1 oz (28.35g)						
CEREALS													
Biscuits, cream crackers	123	517	2.1	3.8	21.4	0.04	0.02	1.0	-	-	-	36	0.5
sweet mixed	148	622	1.6	8.7	18.9	0.04	0.02	0.6	-	-	-	24	0.3
Bread, white	65	73	2.2	0.4	14.9	0.05	-	0.5	-	-	-	26	0.5
Wholemeal	60	252	2.3	0.6	13.4	0.06	0.03	1.0	-	-	-	7.4	0.8
Flour, white	99	416	2.7	0.3	22.3	0.09	-	1.1	-	-	-	42	0.7
wholemeal	89	374	3.7	0.6	18.4	0.13	0.02	2.3	-	-	-	9.8	1.1
Macaroni, boiled	32	134	1.0	0.2	7.2	-	-	0.3	-	-	-	2.3	0.1
Oatmeal, raw	112	470	3.4	2.5	20.6	0.14	0.03	0.3	-	-	-	15.8	1.2
Rice, boiled	35	147	0.6	0.1	8.4	-	-	0.1	-	-	-	0.4	-
Soya, full fat flavour	125	525	11.5	6.7	3.8	0.21	-	0.6	-	-	-	59.3	2.0

Food	Energy		protein	Fat	Carbo-hydrate	Vit B₁	Vit B₂	Nicotinic acid	Vit C	Vit A	Vit D	Calcium	Iron
	kcal	kj	g	G	g	mg	mg	mg	mg	µg	µg	mg	mg
							values per 1 oz (28.35g)						
BEVERAGES													
Cocoa powder	87	365	5.2	6.1	3.2	0.04	0.02	2.0	-	2	-	36	2.9
Coffee, instant	28	118	4.1	-	3.1	-	0.03	7.0	-	-	-	45	1.2
Grapefruit juice, unsweet.	9	38	0.1	-	2.2	0.01	-	0.1	7.8	-	-	3	0.1
Orange juice, unsweet.	9	38	0.1	-	2.4	0.02	0.01	0.1	9.8	2	-	3	0.1
Ribena, undiluted	64	269	-	-	17.1	-	-	-	58.8	-	-	3	0.1
Rosehip syrup, undiluted	65	273	-	-	17.3	-	-	-	82.6	-	-	-	-
Tea, Indian (dry)	30	126	5.5	0.6	0.8	0.04	0.34	2.1	-	-	-	120	4.3
Tomato juice, canned	4	17	0.2	-	0.9	0.02	0.01	0.2	5.6	23	-	3	0.1
FATS AND OILS													
Cod liver oil	252	1058	-	28.0	-	-	-	-	-	5040	59	-	-
Lard	249	1046	-	27.7	-	-	-	-	-	-	-	-	-
Margarine, all kinds	204	857	-	22.7	-	-	-	-	-	252	2.2	1	0.1
Suet, shredded	231	970	-	24.3	3.4	-	-	-	-	18	-	-	-
Vegetable oils	252	1058	-	28.0	-	-	-	-	-	-	-	-	-

Food	Energy		protein	Fat	Carbo-hydrate	Vit B₁	Vit B₂	Nicotinic acid	Vit C	Vit A	Vit D	Calcium	Iron
	kcal	kj	g	G	g	mg	mg values per 1 oz (28.35g)	mg	mg	µg	µg	mg	mg
FISH AND FISH PRODUCTS													
Cod, fried in batter	56	235	5.5	2.9	2.1	-	-	1.0	-	-	-	22	0.1
steamed	23	97	5.2	0.3	-	0.03	0.03	1.6	-	-	-	4	0.1
Fish fingers, fried	65	273	3.8	3.6	4.8	0.02	0.02	1.1	-	-	-	13	0.2
Fish paste	47	197	4.3	2.9	1.0	0.01	0.06	2.0	-	-	-	78	2.5
Haddock, smoked, steamed	28	118	6.5	0.3	-	0.03	0.03	1.7	-	-	-	16	0.3
Plaice, fried in crumbs	64	269	5.0	3.8	2.4	0.06	0.05	1.8	-	-	-	19	0.2
Herring, grilled	56	235	5.7	3.6	-	-	0.05	2.2	-	14	7.0	9	0.3
Kipper, baked	57	239	7.1	3.2	-	-	0.05	2.5	-	14	7.0	18	0.4
Salmon, canned	43	181	5.7	2.3	-	0.01	0.05	3.0	-	25	3.5	26	0.4
Sardines, canned in tomato sauce	50	210	5.0	3.2	0.1	0.01	0.08	2.5	-	-	2.1	129	1.3
FRUIT													
Apples, eating	13	55	0.1	-	3.3	0.01	0.01	-	0.8	1	-	1	0.1
stewed, without sugar	9	38	0.1	-	2.3	0.01	0.01	-	3.4	1	-	1	0.1
Apricots, fresh, raw	9	34	0.2	-	1.9	0.01	0.01	0.2	2.0	70	-	5	0.1
Bananas, raw	22	92	0.3	0.1	5.4	0.01	0.01	0.2	2.8	9.3	-	2	0.1

Food	Energy		protein	Fat	Carbo-hydrate	Vit B₁	Vit B₂	Nicotinic acid	Vit C	Vit A	Vit D	Calcium	Iron
	kcal	kj	g	G	g	mg	mg	mg	mg	µg	µg	mg	mg
							values per 1 oz (28.35g)						
FRUIT cont.													
Blackcurrants, stewed without sugar	7	29	0.2	-	1.6	0.01	0.01	0.1	42.0	8	-	14	0.3
Gooseberries, stewed without sugar	4	17	0.3	-	0.8	0.01	0.01	0.1	8.7	7	-	7	0.1
Grapes, white, raw	18	76	0.2	-	4.5	0.01	0.01	0.1	1.1	-	-	5	0.1
Grapefruit, raw	6	25	0.2	-	1.5	0.01	0.01	0.1	11.2	-	-	5	0.1
Oranges, raw	10	42	0.2	-	2.4	0.03	0.01	0.1	14.0	2	-	11	0.1
Peaches, raw	10	42	0.2	-	2.5	0.01	0.01	0.3	2.2	23	-	1	0.1
Pears, eating	11	46	0.1	-	3.0	0.01	0.01	0.1	0.8	-	-	2	0.1
Pineapple, canned in syrup	22	92	0.1	-	5.7	0.01	0.01	0.1	3.4	2	-	4	0.1
Plums, dessert, raw	11	46	0.2	-	2.7	0.01	0.01	0.2	0.8	10	-	3	0.1
Plums, stewed without sugar	23	97	0.4	-	5.7	0.01	0.03	0.3	-	24	-	5	0.4
Raisins, dried	69	290	0.3	-	18.0	0.03	0.02	0.2	-	1	-	17	0.4
Rhubarb, stewed without sugar	2	8	0.2	-	0.3	-	0.01	0.1	2.2	3	-	26	0.1
Strawberries, raw	7	29	0.2	-	1.7	0.01	0.01	0.1	16.8	1	-	6	0.2

MEAT AND MEAT PRODUCTS

Food	Energy		protein	Fat	Carbo-hydrate	Vit B₁	Vit B₂	Nicotinic acid	Vit C	Vit A	Vit D	Calcium	Iron
	kcal	kj	g	G	g	mg	mg	mg	mg	µg	µg	mg	mg
							values per 1 oz (28.35g)						
Bacon, average rashers, lean, grilled	82	344	8.5	5.3	-	0.16	0.06	3.3	-	-	-	4	0.5
Beef, corned	61	256	7.5	3.4	-	-	0.06	2.5	-	-	-	4	0.8
mince, stewed	64	269	6.5	4.3	-	0.01	0.09	2.6	-	-	-	5	0.9
topside, roast	60	252	7.5	3.4	-	0.02	0.10	3.6	-	-	-	2	0.7
Beefburgers, frozen, fried	74	311	5.7	4.8	2.0	0.01	0.06	2.2	-	-	-	9	0.9
Chicken, roast	41	172	6.9	1.5	-	0.02	0.05	3.6	-	-	-	3	0.2
Ham, canned	34	143	5.2	1.4	-	0.15	0.07	1.9	-	-	-	3	0.3
Kidney, lambs, fried	43	181	6.9	1.8	-	0.16	0.64	4.2	2.5	45	-	4	3.4
Lamb, chops, grilled	99	416	6.6	8.1	-	0.03	0.06	2.8	-	-	-	3	0.5
leg, roast	75	315	7.3	5.0	-	0.03	0.09	3.1	-	-	-	2	0.7
Liver, calves, fried	71	298	7.5	3.7	2.0	0.08	1.18	6.0	3.6	4880	0.1	4	2.1
Pork, chops, grilled	93	391	8.0	6.8	-	0.18	0.06	3.1	-	-	-	3	0.3
leg, roast	80	336	7.5	5.5	-	0.18	0.08	2.8	-	-	-	3	0.4
Sausages, beef, grilled	74	311	3.6	4.8	4.3	-	0.04	2.3	-	-	-	20	0.5
pork, grilled	89	374	3.7	6.9	3.2	0.01	0.04	1.9	-	-	-	15	0.4

Food	Energy		protein	Fat	Carbo-hydrate	Vit B$_1$	Vit B$_2$	Nicotinic acid	Vit C	Vit A	Vit D	Calcium	Iron
	kcal	kj	g	G	g	mg	mg values per 1 oz (28.35g)	mg	mg	µg	µg	mg	mg
MILK PRODUCTS AND EGGS													
Butter, salted	207	869	0.1	24.2	-	-	-	-	-	232	0.2	4	0.1
Cheese, cheddar	114	479	7.2	9.8	-	0.01	0.14	1.7	-	96	0.1	230	0.2
Edam	85	357	6.9	6.5	-	0.01	0.11	1.6	-	67	-	210	-
cottage	27	113	3.8	1.1	0.4	0.06	0.05	0.9	-	10	-	17	-
cream	232	974	0.9	24.5	-	-	0.04	0.2	-	118	0.1	8	-
Cream, single	59	248	0.7	6.0	0.9	0.01	0.03	0.2	0.3	52	-	22	0.1
double	125	525	0.4	13.7	0.6	-	0.02	0.3	0.2	118	0.1	14	0.1
Milk, fresh whole	18	76	0.9	1.0	1.3	0.01	0.05	0.2	0.4	10	-	34	-
condensed, sweetened	90	378	2.3	2.5	15.5	0.02	0.13	0.6	0.6	30	-	78	0.1
evaporated, unsweet.	44	185	2.4	2.5	3.2	0.02	0.14	0.6	0.3	26	0.8	78	0.1
Milk, dried, skimmed	99	416	10.2	0.4	14.8	0.12	0.45	2.7	1.7	-	-	333	0.1
Yoghurt, low fat, natural	15	63	1.4	0.3	1.7	0.01	0.07	0.3	0.1	3	-	50	-
low fat, fruit	27	113	1.3	0.3	5.0	0.01	0.06	0.3	0.5	4	-	45	0.1
Eggs, fresh, whole, raw	41	172	3.4	3.1	-	0.03	0.13	1.0	-	39	0.5	15	0.6

Food	Energy		protein	Fat	Carbo-hydrate	Vit B$_1$	Vit B$_2$	Nicotinic acid	Vit C	Vit A	Vit D	Calcium	Iron
	kcal	kj	g	G	g	mg	mg	mg	mg	µg	µg	mg	mg
							values per 1 oz (28.35g)						
NUTS													
Almonds	158	664	4.7	15.0	1.2	0.07	0.26	1.3	-	-	-	70	1.2
Brazils	173	727	3.4	17.2	1.1	0.28	0.03	1.2	-	-	-	50	0.8
Chestnuts	48	202	0.6	0.8	10.2	0.06	0.06	0.2	-	-	-	13	0.3
Coconut, desiccated	169	710	1.6	17.4	1.8	0.02	0.01	0.5	-	-	-	6	1.0
Hazel	106	445	2.1	10.1	1.9	0.11	-	-	-	-	-	12	0.3
Peanuts, roasted, salted	160	672	6.8	13.7	2.4	0.06	0.03	6.0	-	-	-	17	0.6
Peanut butter	174	731	6.3	15.0	3.7	0.05	0.03	5.6	-	-	-	10	0.6
Walnuts	147	517	3.0	14.4	1.4	0.08	0.04	0.8	-	-	-	17	0.7
SUGAR, PRESERVES AND SWEETS													
Boiled sweets	92	386	-	-	24.4	-	-	-	-	-	-	1	0.1
Chocolate, milk	148	622	2.4	8.5	16.6	0.03	0.06	0.4	-	2	-	62	0.4
plain	147	617	1.3	8.1	18.1	0.02	0.02	0.3	-	2	-	11	0.7
Honey	81	340	0.1	-	21.4	-	0.01	0.1	-	-	-	1	0.1
Jam	73	307	0.2	-	19.3	-	-	-	2.8	-	-	7	0.4
Marmalade	73	307	-	-	19.5	-	-	-	2.8	2	-	10	0.2
Sugar, demerara	110	462	0.1	-	29.3	-	-	-	-	-	-	15	0.3
white	110	462	-	-	29.4	-	-	-	-	-	-	1	-

Food	Energy		protein	Fat	Carbo-hydrate	Vit B₁	Vit B₂	Nicotinic acid	Vit C	Vit A	Vit D	Calcium	Iron
	kcal	kj	g	G	g	mg	mg	mg	mg	µg	µg	mg	mg
							values per 1 oz (28.35g)						

SUGAR, PRESERVES AND SWEETS cont.

Food	kcal	kj	protein	Fat	Carbo-hydrate	Vit B₁	Vit B₂	Nicotinic acid	Vit C	Vit A	Vit D	Calcium	Iron
Syrup, golden	83	349	0.1	-	22.1	-	-	-	-	-	-	7	0.4
Treacle, black	72	302	0.3	-	18.8	-	-	-	-	-	-	140	2.6

VEGETABLES

Food	kcal	kj	protein	Fat	Carbo-hydrate	Vit B₁	Vit B₂	Nicotinic acid	Vit C	Vit A	Vit D	Calcium	Iron
Beans, runner, boiled	5	21	0.5	0.1	0.8	0.01	0.02	0.2	1.4	19	-	6	0.2
broad, boiled	13	55	1.1	0.2	2.0	0.03	0.01	1.0	4.2	12	-	6	0.3
baked, in tomato sauce	18	76	1.4	0.1	2.9	0.02	0.01	0.4	-	-	-	13	0.4
Mung, cooked dahl	30	126	1.8	1.2	3.2	0.03	0.01	0.4	-	19	-	10	0.7
Beetroot, boiled	12	50	0.5	-	2.8	0.01	0.01	0.1	1.4	-	-	8	0.1
Brussels sprouts, boiled	5	21	0.8	-	0.5	0.02	0.03	0.3	11.2	19	-	7	0.1
Cabbage, winter, boiled	4	17	0.5	-	0.6	0.01	0.01	0.1	5.6	14	-	11	0.1
Carrots, old, boiled	5	21	0.2	-	1.2	0.01	0.01	0.1	1.1	560	-	10	0.1
Cauliflower, boiled	3	13	0.4	-	0.2	0.02	0.02	0.2	5.6	1	-	5	0.1
Cucumber, raw	3	13	0.2	-	0.5	0.01	0.01	0.1	2.2	-	-	6	0.1
Leeks, boiled	7	29	0.5	-	1.3	0.02	0.01	0.2	4.2	2	-	17	0.6
Lentils, split, boiled	28	118	2.1	0.1	4.8	0.03	0.01	0.4	-	1	-	4	0.7
Lettuce	3	13	0.3	0.1	0.3	0.02	0.02	0.1	4.2	47	-	6	0.3
Mushrooms, fried	59	248	0.6	6.2	-	0.02	0.10	1.2	0.3	-	-	1	0.4

VEGETABLES cont.

Food	Energy		protein	Fat	Carbo-hydrate	Vit B₁	Vit B₂	Nicotinic acid	Vit C	Vit A	Vit D	Calcium	Iron
	kcal	kj	g	G	g	mg	mg	mg	mg	µg	µg	mg	mg
							values per 1 oz (28.35g)						
Onions, fried	97	407	0.5	9.3	2.8	-	-	0.1	-	-	-	17	0.2
Parsnips, boiled	16	67	0.4	-	3.8	0.02	0.02	0.3	2.8	-	-	10	0.1
Peas, frozen, boiled	11	46	1.5	0.1	1.2	0.07	0.02	0.7	3.6	14	-	36	0.4
chick, cooked, dahl	40	168	2.2	0.9	6.2	0.004	0.01	0.4	0.8	24	-	18	0.9
Plaintin, boiled	34	143	0.3	-	8.7	-	-	0.1	0.8	3	-	3	0.1
Potatoes, boiled	22	92	0.4	-	5.5	0.02	0.01	0.3	3.1	-	-	1	0.1
baked	29	122	0.7	-	7.0	0.03	0.01	0.5	2.8	-	-	3	0.3
roast	44	185	0.8	1.3	7.6	0.03	0.01	0.5	2.8	-	-	3	0.2
chips	71	298	1.1	3.1	10.4	0.03	0.01	0.6	2.8	-	-	4	0.3
crisps	149	626	1.8	10.1	13.8	0.05	0.02	1.7	4.8	-	-	10	0.6
Spinach, boiled	8	34	1.4	0.1	0.4	0.02	0.04	0.5	7.0	280	-	168	1.1
Spring greens, boiled	3	13	0.5	-	0.3	0.02	0.06	0.2	8.4	187	-	24	0.4
Swedes, boiled	5	21	0.3	-	1.1	0.01	0.01	0.3	4.8	-	-	12	0.1
Sweetcorn, canned	21	88	0.8	0.1	4.5	0.01	0.02	0.4	1.4	10	-	1	0.2
Sweet potatoes, boiled	24	101	0.3	0.2	5.6	0.02	0.01	0.3	4.2	187	-	6	0.2
Tomatoes, raw	4	17	0.3	-	0.8	0.02	0.01	0.2	5.6	28	-	4	0.1
Turnips, boiled	4	17	0.2	0.1	0.6	0.01	0.01	0.2	4.8	-	-	15	0.1
Yam, boiled	33	139	0.4	-	8.3	0.01	-	0.2	0.6	1	-	3	0.1

BABY FOOD

In this section I have tried to give an adequate amount of recipes to work from, but please try experimenting by adding other milk- and egg-free dishes with different tastes and textures to your baby's menu. Also include plenty of fresh fruit and vegetables in your baby's diet.

Introduce any new foods to your baby gradually, starting with very small quantities. Never force your baby to eat something they dislike. Find another food to fulfil the dietary role of the rejected food.

Cereals should not be added to bottles of milk. They should be given to your baby, mixed with the recommended milk-free feed, by spoon.

Fresh fruit and vegetable juices make a nutritious and pleasant drink, but for a young baby dilute the juice by half.

Never use salt in food for babies under 9 months.

For sandwich fillings and spreads which can be used for babies, see pages 77–79.

All these recipes, except the rusks, are designed to make one serving.

BABY MILK

The term 'baby milk' used in the following recipes, means whatever milk your baby is having. It is most important that you continue feeding your baby with the fortified milk-free feed recommended by your doctor or dietician.

Do not give Basic soya-milk or Super creamy milk-free milk to babies under weaning age.

29

Before making any changes to your baby's diet, always check with your doctor or dietician first.

PREPARATION OF UTENSILS

All utensils, including the liquidiser, used in preparing, cooking and serving baby foods should be washed thoroughly, rinsed and sterilised before each use.

APPLE AND PEANUT BUTTER

	Metric	Imperial	American
Eating apple, peeled and cored	1 small	1 small	1 small
Peanut butter	½ tbsp	½ tbsp	½ tbsp
A little apple juice if desired			

Place all the ingredients in a liquidiser and blend on maximum speed until the desired consistency is reached. Spoon feed, or serve on bread or rusks.

30

BEEF AND VEGETABLE DINNER

	Metric	Imperial	American
Cooked beef	50 g	2 oz	2 oz
Mashed potato	25 g	1 oz	1/8 cup
Cooked vegetables	25 g	1 oz	1 oz
Gravy	1–2 tbsp	1–2 tbsp	1–2 tbsp

Place all the ingredients in a liquidiser and blend on maximum speed until the desired consistency. Remove and pour into a saucepan. Cook over a low heat for 10 minutes.

Cooking time: 10 minutes.

BACON AND BEANS

	Metric	Imperial	American
Lean bacon	2 rashers	2 rashers	2 rashers
Baked beans	75 g	3 oz	1/2 cup

Trim any excess fat from bacon. Grill lightly. Chop the bacon into tiny pieces. Heat the beans. Remove from the heat and mix with the bacon.

Cooking time: 5–10 minutes.

Note: This can be liquidised for a small baby.

MEXICAN MINCE

	Metric	Imperial	American
Cooked lean mince, beef or lamb	50 g	2 oz	2 oz
Finely chopped onion	½ tbsp	½ tbsp	½ tbsp
Cooked red kidney beans	1 tbsp	1 tbsp	1 tbsp
Cooked peas	1 tbsp	1 tbsp	1 tbsp
Tomato purée	1-2 tsp	1-2 tsp	1-2 tsp
Meat or vegetable stock	4-5 tbsp	4-5 tbsp	4-5 tbsp
A few drops vegetable oil			

Heat the oil and cook the onion in it until soft and translucent. Add the mince, vegetables, tomato purée and stock. Mix well. Cook thoroughly over a medium heat. Liquidise for a small baby.

Cooking time: 15-20 minutes.

STEAMED CHICKEN DINNER

	Metric	Imperial	American
Sliced breast of chicken	50 g	2 oz	2 oz
Water	1-2 tbsp	1-2 tbsp	1-2 tbsp

Put the chicken breast in a Tomor-greased soup dish. Add the water. Cover with a plate and steam gently over boiling water until cooked.

Serve with vegetables or baby rice. Liquidise for a small baby.

Cooking time: 15-20 minutes.

CARROTS IN CREAMY PARSLEY

	Metric	Imperial	American
Carrots, sliced	1	1	1
Lemon juice			
Parsley, chopped	½ tsp	½ tsp	½ tsp
Baby milk			

Place the carrots in unsalted boiling water and simmer for about 15 minutes or until tender. Drain. Mix the carrot slices with a drop of lemon juice and the parsley. Place in a liquidiser and blend with a little baby milk.

Cooking time: 15 minutes.

PEAS WITH RICE

	Metric	Imperial	American
Peas, shelled or frozen	1 tbsp	1 tbsp	1 tbsp
Brown rice, cooked	1 tbsp	1 tbsp	1 tbsp
Baby milk			

Put the peas in a saucepan, cover with boiling water and simmer for about 20 minutes (follow manufacturer's instructions for frozen peas) or until the peas are tender. Drain and mix in the rice. Place in a liquidiser and blend with a little baby milk.

Cooking time: 20 minutes.

CREAMED FISH DINNER

	Metric	Imperial	American
Fish	1 small piece	1 small piece	1 small piece
Baby milk or Super creamy milk-free milk (page 146)	1 tbsp	1 tbsp	1 tbsp
Pinch of salt			
Milk-free savoury white sauce (page 137)	1 tbsp	1 tbsp	1 tbsp

Place the fish in a Tomor greased soup dish. Add the milk and a little salt. Cover with a plate and steam gently over boiling water until cooked. Remove the bones and skin. Mix the fish with the milk-free white sauce. Beat well and serve.

Cooking time: 10 minutes.

LAMB AND VEGETABLE DINNER

	Metric	Imperial	American
Cooked lamb	50 g	2 oz	2 oz
Cooked peas	25 g	1 oz	1 oz
Raw carrot, grated	25 g	1 oz	1 oz
Meat stock	6–7 tbsp	6–7 tbsp	6–7 tbsp

Place all the ingredients in a liquidiser and blend on maximum speed until the desired consistency. Remove and pour into a saucepan. Cook over a low heat for 10 minutes.

Cooking time: 10 minutes.

TURKEY AND VEGETABLE DINNER

	Metric	Imperial	American
Cooked turkey	50 g	2 oz	2 oz
Cooked vegetables	25 g	1 oz	1 oz
Baby milk or Super creamy milk-free milk (page 146)	6–7 tbsp	6–7 tbsp	6–7 tbsp
Potato	25 g	1 oz	1/8 cup

Place all the ingredients in a liquidiser and blend on maximum speed until the desired consistency. Remove and pour into a saucepan. Cook over a low heat for 10 minutes.

Cooking time: 10 minutes.

Variation: For **Turkey dinner with rice**, replace the potato with 1–2 teaspoons of Robinson's baby rice.

BACON AND VEGETABLE DINNER

	Metric	Imperial	American
Lean bacon	2 rashers	2 rashers	2 rashers
Mashed potato	25 g	1 oz	1/8 cup
Cooked vegetables	25 g	1 oz	1 oz
Gravy	1½ tbsp	1½ tbsp	1½ tbsp

Trim any excess fat from the bacon. Grill lightly and chop into small pieces. Place the bacon, vegetables and gravy in the liquidiser. Blend on maximum speed until the desired consistency. Remove and pour into a saucepan. Cook over a low heat for 10 minutes.

Cooking time: 10 minutes.

MINCED LIVER

	Metric	Imperial	American
Liver	25 g	1 oz	1 oz
Milk-free savoury white sauce (page 137)	1–2 tbsp	1–2 tbsp	1–2 tbsp
Salt and pepper			

Mince the liver and place in a soup dish. Mix in the milk-free white sauce and season lightly. Cover with a plate and steam gently over boiling water until barely cooked. Serve with mashed potatoes and vegetables.

Cooking time: 10–15 minutes.

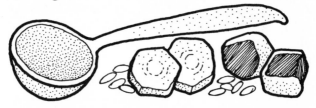

CREAMED HERRING ROE

	Metric	Imperial	American
Herring roe	1	1	1
Baby milk or Super creamy milk-free milk (page 146)	1½ tbsp	1½ tbsp	1½ tbsp
Cornflour	1 tsp	1 tsp	1 tsp
Pinch of salt			

Wash the herring roe. Place in a saucepan with a tablespoon of milk. Cook gently for 5 minutes. Put the cornflour into a cup and blend with half a tablespoon of milk until smooth. When the roe has cooked for 5 minutes, season with salt and mash well with a fork. Add the cornflour. Return to the heat and cook slowly for a few minutes until the cornflour has cooked.

Serve with baby rice or mashed potatoes.

Cooking time: 10 minutes.

FISH FINGERS

	Metric	Imperial	American
Potatoes	75 g	3 oz	3 oz
Fish, cod or haddock	50 g	2 oz	2 oz
Fresh parsley, washed and chopped	1-2 tsp	1-2 tsp	1-2 tsp
Fresh breadcrumbs			

Peel the potatoes and boil for 20 minutes. Place the fish in a Tomor-greased soup dish and steam over a pan of boiling water for 10 minutes. When cooked, flake the fish and remove the bones. Drain and mash the potatoes. Mix the fish, parsley and potatoes together. Form into fingers and coat each finger with breadcrumbs. Grill for a few minutes.

Cooking time: 25 minutes.

SAVOURY RUSKS

	Metric	Imperial	American
Water	150 ml	1/4 pt	2/3 cup
Marmite	1/2 tsp	1/2 tsp	1/2 tsp
Bread	4 thick slices	4 thick slices	4 thick slices

Put the water and marmite into a saucepan. Cook over a low heat until the marmite has dissolved. Cut the bread into fingers and dip each one into the mixture. Arrange on a baking tray and dry out in a very cool oven, 110°C/225°F/Gas mark 1/4.

HONEY RUSKS

	Metric	Imperial	American
Water	150 ml	¼ pt	⅔ cup
Honey	2 tsp	2 tsp	2 tsp
Bread	4 thick slices	4 thick slices	4 thick slices

Put the water and honey into a saucepan. Cook over a low heat until the honey has dissolved. Cut the bread into fingers and dip each one into the honey and water mixture. Arrange on a baking tray and dry out in a very cool oven, 110°C/225°F/ Gas mark ¼.

CHOCOLATE CREAM DESSERT

	Metric	Imperial	American
Soya flour	1 tbsp	1 tbsp	1 tbsp
Drinking chocolate	1 tsp	1 tsp	1 tsp
Boiling water	2 tbsp	2 tbsp	2 tbsp

Put the soya flour and drinking chocolate in a dish. Mix to a smooth paste with the boiling water. Cool.

Note: See page 9 on the use of coconut and cocoa products.

BANANA DESSERT

	Metric	Imperial	American
Banana	1	1	1
Honey	1 tsp	1 tsp	1 tsp
Baby milk or Super creamy milk-free milk (page 146)	2 tbsp	2 tbsp	2 tbsp

Chop the banana and place in the liquidiser. Add the milk and honey. Blend on minimum speed.

PEAR AND CUSTARD DESSERT

	Metric	Imperial	American
Stewed pear	1	1	1
Milk-free creamy custard (page 142)	2–3 tbsp	2–3 tbsp	2–3 tbsp
Honey	1 tsp	1 tsp	1 tsp

Place the pear and custard in the liquidiser. Blend on minimum speed for 1 minute. Add the honey and serve.

Variations: Use stewed dried apricots, rhubarb, plums, or any fruit, fresh or stewed.

PRUNE AND HONEY DESSERT

	Metric	Imperial	American
Prunes	3	3	3
Honey	1 tsp	1 tsp	1 tsp

Cook and stone the prunes. Place in the liquidiser with a little of the liquid in which the prunes have been cooked. Blend on minimum speed for about 1 minute. Stir in the honey and serve.

BLACKCURRANT CREAM

	Metric	Imperial	American
Soya flour	1 tbsp	1 tbsp	1 tbsp
Boiling water	2 tbsp	2 tbsp	2 tbsp
Blackcurrant juice	½ tsp	½ tsp	½ tsp

Put the soya flour in a dish. Mix to a smooth paste with the boiling water. Cool. Add the black-currant juice and mix well.

Variations: Use orange juice or rose hip syrup instead of blackcurrant juice.

FRUIT AND MAPLE SYRUP DESSERT

	Metric	Imperial	American
Banana	½	½	½
Eating apple, peeled cored and finely grated	½	½	½
Maple syrup	1-2 tsp	1-2 tsp	1-2 tsp

Mash the banana with a fork. Add the grated apple and maple syrup. Mix well. Liquidise for a small baby.

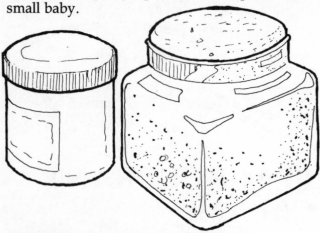

ORANGE AND MELON PURÉE

	Metric	Imperial	American
Orange	½	½	½
Honey dew melon	1 thin slice	1 thin slice	1 thin slice

Peel the orange and remove the pith and pips. Slice the melon and remove the peel and seeds. Place in a liquidiser and blend on minimum speed for 1 minute.

CREAM OF TOMATO SOUP

	Metric	Imperial	American
Tomor	14 g	½ oz	1 tbsp
Onion, chopped	1 small	1 small	1 small
Streaky bacon	1 rasher	1 rasher	1 rasher
Potato, sliced	1 medium	1 medium	1 medium
Fresh tomatoes, sliced	450 g	1 lb	1 lb
Celery, chopped	1 stick	1 stick	1 stick
Sugar	½ tsp	½ tsp	½ tsp
Water	150 ml	¼ pt	⅔ cup
Salt	1 tsp	1 tsp	1 tsp
Cayenne pepper	¼ tsp	¼ tsp	¼ tsp
Super creamy milk-free milk (page 146)	150 ml	¼ pt	⅔ cup
Chopped parsley for garnish			

Melt the Tomor in a saucepan. Add the onion and bacon, and cook gently for about 5 minutes. Add the potato, tomatoes, celery, sugar and water. Cover the saucepan and simmer gently until the potato is cooked. Then remove the bacon and pour the soup into a liquidiser. Season with salt and cayenne pepper. Blend until smooth. Add the super creamy milk, and blend again. Return to the saucepan and reheat gently. Serve sprinkled with chopped parsley.

Cooking time: 20 minutes.

WATERCRESS SOUP

	Metric	Imperial	American
Tomor	50 g	2 oz	¼ cup
Onion, chopped	1 medium	1 medium	1 medium
Watercress, chopped	75 g	3 oz	3 oz
Leek soup (page 45)	600 ml	1 pt	2½ cups
Salt and pepper			

Melt 25 g/1 oz/2 tbsp of Tomor in a saucepan. Add the onion and watercress and cook gently for a few minutes. Place in a liquidiser and blend until finely chopped. Return to the saucepan. Add the Leek soup. Season with salt and pepper. Simmer gently for about 5 minutes. Add the remaining Tomor and serve.

Cooking time: 10 minutes.

AUTUMN POTAGE

	Metric	Imperial	American
Potatoes, sliced	4 medium	4 medium	4 medium
Leeks, sliced	3 medium	3 medium	3 medium
Frozen peas	4 tbsp	4 tbsp	4 tbsp
Celery, chopped	2–3 sticks	2–3 sticks	2–3 sticks
Red pepper, deseeded and chopped	½ small	½ small	½ small
Water	1.1 l	2 pt	5 cups
Tomor	15 g	½ oz	1 tbsp
Salt and pepper			

Place the vegetables and water in a saucepan and cook for about 10 minutes. Pour into a liquidiser and blend until smooth. Return to the pan, add the Tomor and season with salt and pepper. Reheat and stir well before serving.

Cooking time: 15 minutes.

LEEK SOUP

	Metric	Imperial	American
Potatoes	*5 medium*	*5 medium*	*5 medium*
Leeks, sliced	*3 medium*	*3 medium*	*3 medium*
Water	*900 ml*	*1½ pt*	*3¾ cups*
Tomor	*15 g*	*½ oz*	*1 tbsp*
Salt and pepper			
Chopped chives for garnish			

Peel the potatoes and cut in half. Then place in a saucepan with the leeks and water and cook for about 10 minutes. Pour into a liquidiser and blend until smooth. Return to the pan, add the Tomor, season with salt and pepper. Reheat. Sprinkle with chopped chives before serving.

Cooking time: 15 minutes.

LENTIL SOUP

	Metric	Imperial	American
Lentils	225 g	8 oz	1 cup
Tomor	25 g	1 oz	2 tbsp
Onion, chopped	1	1	1
Bacon	1 rasher	1 rasher	1 rasher
Carrot, sliced	1	1	1
Turnip, chopped into small pieces	1 small	1 small	1 small
Water	900 ml	1½ pt	3¾ cups
Parsley	1 tbsp	1 tbsp	1 tbsp
Thyme	1 tbsp	1 tbsp	1 tbsp
Salt and pepper			

Place the lentils in a liquidiser and grind for 1 minute. Melt the Tomor in a saucepan, add the onion and bacon and cook until golden brown. Next, add the carrot and turnip and cook for a few minutes, stirring frequently. Add the ground lentils, water, parsley and thyme. Slowly bring to the boil. Cover and simmer gently for 45 minutes. Pour into the liquidiser and blend until smooth. Return to the pan. Season with salt and pepper. Reheat and serve.

Cooking time: 45 minutes.

Variation: For **Split pea soup**, follow the same recipe using split peas instead of lentils.

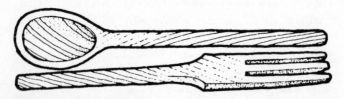

FISH

When choosing fresh fish, look for a firm fish with bright gills and scales. The flesh should be firm and the eyes bright. Avoid fish that has a chemical odour. Fresh fish has a pleasant smell.

BAKED FISH CRUMBLE

	Metric	Imperial	American
Flour	1 tbsp	1 tbsp	1 tbsp
Salt and pepper			
Cod or haddock	680 g	1½ lb	1½ lb
Super creamy milk-free milk (page 146)	4 tbsp	4 tbsp	4 tbsp
Tomatoes, sliced	225 g	8 oz	½ lb
Tomor	100 g	4 oz	½ cup
Porridge oats	225 g	8 oz	2⅔ cups
Dried mixed herbs	1 tsp	1 tsp	1 tsp

Season the flour with the salt and pepper. Skin the fish, cut into small chunks and coat with the flour. Place the fish in an oven-proof dish and sprinkle with the rest of the flour. Pour on the milk and cover the fish with the tomato slices.

Melt the Tomor in a saucepan. Stir in the porridge oats and dried herbs. When mixed, remove from the heat and place over the fish. Press the mixture down firmly. Bake at 190°C/375°F/Gas mark 5 for 40 minutes until the crumble turns brown.

Cooking time: 40 minutes.

STEAMED HADDOCK IN LEMON CREAMY SAUCE

	Metric	Imperial	American
Haddock (or any other white fish)	4 slices	4 slices	4 slices
Salt and pepper			
Tomor	50 g	2 oz	¼ cup
Flour	2 tbsp	2 tbsp	2 tbsp
Super creamy milk-free milk (page 146)	150 ml	¼ pt	⅔ cup
Water	150 ml	¼ pt	⅔ cup
Juice and grated rind of 1 lemon			

Season the fish with salt and pepper. Place a sliver of Tomor on each side, wrap in greaseproof paper and steam for 15 minutes. If you have no steamer, grease two plates with Tomor and place the fish between them. Cook over a pan of boiling water for 15 minutes.

While the fish is cooking, make the sauce. Put the flour into a saucepan over a low heat. Pour in a little of the milk and blend to a smooth paste. Then add the remaining milk and water. Stir continuously until the sauce thickens. Add the lemon juice and rind. When the fish is cooked, pour the sauce over the fish and serve.

Cooking time: 15 minutes.

Variation: One large piece of fish can be cooked in the same way, but allow a little longer time.

GRILLED KIPPERS WITH PARSLEY BUTTER

	Metric	Imperial	American
Tomor	75 g	3 g	⅓ cup
Chopped parsley	1 tbsp	1 tbsp	1 tbsp
Black pepper			
Kippers	2	2	2
Lemon	6 slices	6 slices	6 slices

Slightly soften the Tomor and blend with the parsley and pepper. Chill. Place the kippers in a dish. Cover them with boiling water and leave for a few minutes until tender. Remove and brush with a little melted Tomor parsley butter. Heat the grill. Place the kippers under the grill to crisp slightly. Remove and garnish with the sliced lemon and the remaining Tomor parsley butter.

Cooking time: 5 minutes.

WHITEBAIT

	Metric	Imperial	American
Whitebait	225 g	8 oz	½ lb
Plain flour	25 g	1 oz	¼ cup
Salt and pepper			
Lemon juice			

Season the flour with the salt and pepper. Rinse the fish with cold water, pat dry and toss in the seasoned flour. Fry in very hot oil or fat for 3–4 minutes. When cooked, drain on absorbent paper. Sprinkle liberally with fresh lemon juice before serving.

Cooking time: 3–4 minutes.

TROUT WITH SESAME SEEDS

	Metric	Imperial	American
Trout	4	4	4
Tomor			
Oatmeal	2 tbsp	2 tbsp	2 tbsp
Salt and pepper			
Sesame seeds, toasted	25 g	1 oz	¼ cup

Slit, clean and remove the heads from the trout. Dry thoroughly. Well grease an oven-proof casserole dish with Tomor. Season the oatmeal with salt and pepper, then roll the trout in it. Place the fish side by side in the casserole. Sprinkle with sesame seeds. Cover and bake at 190°C/375°F/Gas mark 5 for 30 minutes. Then remove the lid and allow to brown for a further 10 minutes.

Cooking time: 40 minutes.

CRUNCHY FRIED HERRINGS IN OATMEAL

	Metric	Imperial	American
Herrings	4	4	4
Oatmeal	2 tbsp	2 tbsp	2 tbsp
Salt and pepper			
Tomor	25 g	1 oz	2 tbsp
Lemon slices for garnish			

Scale the herrings. Cut off the heads and tails, slit open and clean (or ask the fishmonger to do this for you). Wash and dry. Season the oatmeal with salt and pepper then roll the fish in it. Heat the Tomor in a frying pan. Fry the fish for about 8 minutes, turning once. Serve with slices of lemon.

Cooking time: 8 minutes.

SMOKED HADDOCK FLAN

	Metric	Imperial	American
Milk-free shortcrust pastry (page 133)	175 g	6 oz	6 oz
Smoked haddock	450 g	1 lb	1 lb
Water			
Tomor	75 g	3 oz	⅓ cup
Button mushrooms	225 g	8 oz	½ lb
Flour	3 tbsp	3 tbsp	3 tbsp
Chives, chopped	1 tbsp	1 tbsp	1 tbsp
Lemon juice	1 tsp	1 tsp	1 tsp
Salt and pepper			
Parsley and lemon slices for garnish			

Heat the oven. Roll out the pastry and line a flan dish. Prick the base lightly and bake blind at 200°C/400°F/Gas mark 6 for about 25 minutes.

Rinse the smoked haddock with water and place in an oven-proof dish. Cover with water. Poach gently for about 10 minutes until the fish is cooked, then drain the fish stock into a jug and keep for the sauce. Flake the fish into a bowl.

Melt 50 g/2 oz/¼ cup of the Tomor in a saucepan. Fry the mushrooms quickly. Remove from the heat and mix with the fish. Melt the remaining Tomor in the pan and blend in the flour. Now measure 300 ml/½ pt/1¼ cups of the fish stock and pour a little at a time into the flour and Tomor. Mix well. Bring slowly to the boil and simmer for 2–3 minutes. Remove from the heat and allow to cool. When cool, add the sauce to the fish mixture. Sprinkle in the chives. Add the lemon juice and season with salt and pepper. Mix well. Fill the flan case and garnish.

Cooking time: 50 minutes.

SAVOURY FISH CASSEROLE

	Metric	Imperial	American
White fish	4 slices	4 slices	4 slices
Oil	4 tbsp	4 tbsp	4 tbsp
Onion	1	1	1
Green pepper	1	1	1
Sugar	2 tsp	2 tsp	2 tsp
Tomatoes	340 g	12 oz	¾ lb
Salt and pepper			
Flour	1 tbsp	1 tbsp	1 tbsp
Lemon juice	1 tbsp	1 tbsp	1 tbsp
Courgettes	100 g	4 oz	¼ lb

Wash the fish and place in an oven-proof casserole dish with the oil. Peel the onion, wash the green pepper and remove the seeds. Place the sugar, tomatoes, salt, pepper, flour and lemon juice into a liquidiser and blend at maximum speed for 10 seconds. Then add the courgettes, onion and green pepper. Blend until coarsely chopped. Pour the mixture over the fish and bake at 180°C/350°F/Gas mark 4 for about 25 minutes.

Cooking time: 25 minutes.

LE COURT-BOUILLON COLIE

	Metric	Imperial	American
Carrot	1 large	1 large	1 large
Celery	2 sticks	2 sticks	2 sticks
Cloves	12	12	12
Onion	1 large	1 large	1 large
Pinch of salt			
Twist of black pepper			
Bay leaves	3	3	3
Vinegar	1–2 tbsp	1–2 tbsp	1–2 tbsp
Coley or hake	1 large or 4 small	1 large or 4 small	1 large or 4 small

Wash and peel the vegetables. Press the cloves firmly into the whole peeled onion. Place the vegetables, herbs, spices and vinegar into a saucepan, just cover with cold water and simmer gently for 1 hour.

Next clean the fish and place in a fish kettle or large oven-proof dish. When ready, pour the liquid over the fish, keeping the vegetables aside. Place in the oven and cook for 20–30 minutes for a large fish, 10–15 for small. When cooked, drain off the liquid. Allow the fish to cool completely before eating. Serve with the vegetables.

This dish is delicious served on a summer evening, generously sprinkled with lemon juice, accompanied by new potatoes tossed in Mint or

Parsley butter (pages 85–6) and fresh asparagus with French dressing (page 81).

Cooking time: 20–30 minutes.

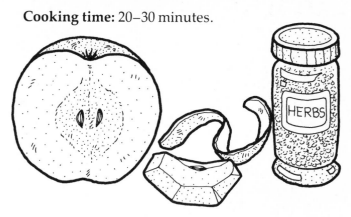

COD WITH APPLES

	Metric	Imperial	American
Onion, finely chopped	*1*	*1*	*1*
Cooking apples, finely chopped	*4*	*4*	*4*
Celery heart, chopped	*1*	*1*	*1*
Cod or haddock steaks	*4*	*4*	*4*
Salt and pepper			
Water	*300 ml*	*½ pt*	*1¼ cups*

Place the chopped onion, apples and celery in an oven-proof casserole dish. Top with the fish and season well. Pour the water over the fish. Cover and bake at 180°C/350°F/Gas mark 4 for 35–45 minutes until the vegetables are cooked.

Cooking time: 35–45 minutes.

PICKLED HERRINGS

	Metric	Imperial	American
Fresh herrings, boned	6	6	6
Vinegar	600 ml	1 pt	2½ cups
Water	150 ml	¼ pt	⅔ cup
Pickling spice	1 tsp	1 tsp	1 tsp
Salt			
Onions, cut into rings	2	2	2
Pure cane syrup	1 tsp	1 tsp	1 tsp
Cornflour	1 tsp	1 tsp	1 tsp

Slit open and clean the herrings (or ask the fishmonger to do this for you) and place in an oven-proof dish. Cover with the vinegar and water. Add the spice, salt and onions. Mix the syrup in 2 teaspoonfuls of warm water and pour this over the herrings. Now blend the cornflour with 2 tablespoons of cold water and add it to the liquid in the dish. Mix well. Bake at 140°C/275°F/Gas mark 1 until soft.

Cooking time: 1 hour.

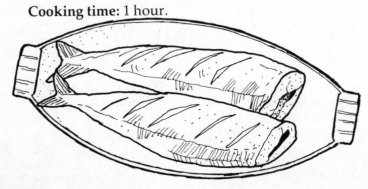

MEAT, PASTA AND SAVOURY

Here are a few tips to remember when buying fresh meat.

Beef. To choose good quality beef, look for meat which is firm to the touch. The flesh should be bright red with a brownish tinge. The lean should contain small flecks of fat, known as 'marbling', and the prime cuts should be free of gristle.

Lamb. When buying lamb, the colour of the flesh will vary from pink for a very young lamb to a dark red, depending on the age and variety of sheep. Look for a moist pink flesh and firm, white fat. Brittle white and yellowish fat should be avoided.

Leg and shoulders should be plump, with a blue tinge on the knuckle bones. A layer of fat should cover both, indicating the animal is young.

Pork. To recognise good quality pork one should look for firm, smooth, lean flesh with firm white fat. The lean should contain small flecks of fat, known as 'marbling'.

Bacon. Bacon is extremely versatile and relatively inexpensive; with it one can make a wide variety of dishes. When choosing bacon, look for firm flesh, deep pink in colour or good bright red with firm white fat. Avoid bacon that has any yellow or greenish stains.

EGGLESS MINCEMEAT LOAF

	Metric	Imperial	American
Onion, chopped	1 small	1 small	1 small
Tomor	25 g	1 oz	2 tbsp
Minced beef	450 g	1 lb	1 lb
Fresh breadcrumbs or rolled oats	40 g	1½ oz	½ cup
Ground nutmeg	¼ tsp	¼ tsp	¼ tsp
Salt	1 tsp	1 tsp	1 tsp
Pepper	¼ tsp	¼ tsp	¼ tsp
Garlic, crushed	1–2 cloves	1–2 cloves	1–2 cloves
Super creamy milk-free milk (page 146) or stock	4–8 tbsp	4–8 tbsp	4–8 tbsp
Fresh or dried herbs, chopped			

Heat the oven. Fry the onion in a little Tomor. Mix all the ingredients together, with seasoning to taste, working until smooth, adding liquid as needed to make it hold together. Turn on to a floured board, flour your hands and shape the meat into a loaf about 8 cm/3 in deep. Melt a little Tomor in a roasting tin, add the loaf and cover with a piece of foil. Bake at 190°C/375°F/Gas mark 5 for ¾–1 hour, removing the foil for the last 10 minutes.

Serve hot with gravy or Tomato sauce (page 76) with potatoes and any vegetable; or serve cold with salad and pickles; or use as a sandwich filling.

Cooking time: ¾–1 hour.

LAMB CASSEROLE WITH APPLE JUICE

	Metric	Imperial	American
Lean lamb (boneless)	900 g	2 lb	2 lb
Flour	1 tbsp	1 tbsp	1 tbsp
Tomor	50 g	2 oz	¼ cup
Onions, chopped	2 small	2 small	2 small
Parsley, chopped	2 tbsp	2 tbsp	2 tbsp
Stock	150 ml	¼ pt	⅔ cup
Apple juice	150 ml	¼ pt	⅔ cup
Worcester sauce	1 tbsp	1 tbsp	1 tbsp
Salt	1 tsp	1 tsp	1 tsp
Pepper	½ tsp	½ tsp	½ tsp

Cut the meat into small pieces and toss in the flour. Heat the Tomor in a frying pan and fry the meat until brown. Remove and place in a casserole with the chopped onions and parsley. Pour the stock and apple juice into the frying pan and stir until boiling. Add the Worcester sauce and seasoning and cook for 5 minutes. Remove from the heat and pour over the meat. Cook at 170°C/325°F/Gas mark 3 for about 1½ hours.

Cooking time: 1½ hours.

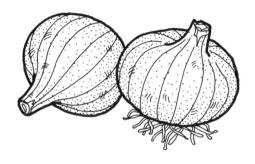

APPLE AND BACON PIE

	Metric	Imperial	American
Milk-free shortcrust pastry (page 133)	175 g	6 oz	6 oz
Lean sliced bacon	450 g	1 lb	1 lb
Cooking apples	225 g	8 oz	½ lb
Onions	75 g	3 oz	3 oz
Salt and pepper			
Water			

Make the pastry. Cut the bacon into small pieces. Peel and slice the apples and onions. Put a layer of bacon in the pie dish, then a layer of onions and finally apple. Season well with salt and pepper. Repeat the layers until all is used. Add cold water to come half way up the dish. Cover with the pastry and cut a hole in the centre. Bake at 230°C/450°F/Gas mark 8 for 15 minutes, then reduce the heat to 190°C/375°F/Gas mark 5 for a further 30–45 minutes.

Cooking time: ¾–1 hour.

PASTA SURPRISE

	Metric	Imperial	American
Egg-free spaghetti	225 g	8 oz	½ lb
Bacon rashers	225 g	8 oz	½ lb
Canned tomatoes	400 g	14 oz	14 oz
Dried mixed herbs	1 tsp	1 tsp	1 tsp
Salt and pepper			

Cook the spaghetti as directed. Grill or fry the bacon, cut into small pieces. Heat the tomatoes in a saucepan and add half the bacon. Add the mixed herbs and season well. Drain the spaghetti and place on a warm dish. Pour the bacon and tomato sauce over. Top with the remaining bacon.

Cooking time: 20 minutes.

PORK CHOPS WITH SAVOURY RICE

	Metric	Imperial	American
Pork chops, trimmed of fat	4	4	4
Sage	1 tsp	1 tsp	1 tsp
Onions, chopped	2 small	2 small	2 small
Salt and pepper			
Canned tomatoes	400 g	14 oz	14 oz
Canned sweetcorn with peppers	340 g	12 oz	¾ lb
Rice	340 g	12 oz	1½ cups
Chilli powder	½ tsp	½ tsp	½ tsp

Place the pork chops in the bottom of an oven-proof casserole dish. Sprinkle on the sage, cover with onions and season to taste. Mix the rest of the ingredients together and pour over the chops. Cover and bake at 150°C/300°F/Gas mark 2 for 1–1½ hours.

Cooking time: 1–1½ hours.

BEEF CURRY

	Metric	Imperial	American
Chuck steak	900 g	2 lb	2 lb
Flour	50 g	2 oz	½ cup
Salt	3 tsp	3 tsp	3 tsp
Onions	2 medium	2 medium	2 medium
Apples	2	2	2
Tomato	1	1	1
Garlic	½ clove	½ clove	½ clove
Tomor	50 g	2 oz	¼ cup
Curry powder	2 tbsp	2 tbsp	2 tbsp
Stock	425 ml	¾ pt	2 cups
Juice and grated rind of ½ lemon			
Sultanas	2 tbsp	2 tbsp	2 tbsp
Molasses sugar	1 tsp	1 tsp	1 tsp
Desiccated coconut	1 tbsp	1 tbsp	1 tbsp

Cut the meat into small pieces, roll it in the flour seasoned with salt. Peel and slice onions, apples and tomato. Crush the garlic. Heat the Tomor in a saucepan and fry the meat in it. When brown, add the vegetables, apples and tomatoes and fry for 2 minutes. Pour off any excess fat. Add the curry powder and any flour left after coating the meat. Mix well and stir in the stock. Add the remaining ingredients and simmer for 2–3 hours on top of the cooker or for 20 minutes in a pressure cooker.

Serve with rice and sliced green peppers.

Cooking time: 2–3 hours.

Variation: Lamb curry can be made in the same way.

Note: Canned curry may contain egg albumen.

See page 9 on the use of coconut and cocoa products.

A curry can be kept hot for a long time without spoiling. It can be made the day before and re-heated, but be sure to bring it to the boil before serving.

HERB LAMB PATTIES

	Metric	Imperial	American
Lean lamb	450 g	1 lb	1 lb
Parsley, chopped	½ tbsp	½ tbsp	½ tbsp
Dried mixed herbs	½ tsp	½ tsp	½ tsp
Salt and pepper			
Streaky bacon	4 rashers	4 rashers	4 rashers

Mince the lamb, add the herbs and season with salt and pepper. Mix well. Divide into 4 equal portions and form into flat rounds. Wrap a rasher of bacon around each pattie and secure with a cocktail stick. Grill slowly for about 25 minutes, turning once. Serve immediately.

Cooking time: 25 minutes.

LIVER WITH GREEN PEPPERS

	Metric	Imperial	American
Plain flour	2 tbsp	2 tbsp	2 tbsp
Salt and pepper			
Ox liver, sliced	450 g	1 lb	1 lb
Tomor	25 g	1 oz	2 tbsp
Onions, sliced	2 medium	2 medium	2 medium
Green peppers, deseeded and thinly sliced	2	2	2
Fresh tomatoes, skinned	450 g	1 lb	1 lb

Season the flour with salt and pepper and lightly coat the liver slices. Melt the Tomor in a pan and fry the liver a few pieces at a time until lightly browned on both sides. Remove as they brown and keep warm. Add the onion, green peppers and tomatoes to the pan. Season. Return the liver to the pan. Cover and simmer gently for about 20 minutes.

Cooking time: 20 minutes.

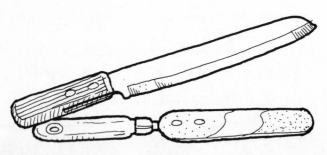

RABBIT AND MUSHROOM PIE

	Metric	Imperial	American
Flour	1 tbsp	1 tbsp	1 tbsp
Salt and pepper			
Rabbit, jointed	1	1	1
Tomor	25 g	1 oz	2 tbsp
Onion, chopped	1 large	1 large	1 large
Streaky bacon, chopped	225 g	8 oz	½ lb
Mushrooms, chopped	100 g	4 oz	¼ lb
Stock	300 ml	½ pt	1¼ cups
Milk-free shortcrust pastry (page 133)	225 g	8 oz	½ lb

Mix the flour, salt and pepper together and coat each rabbit joint. Put the Tomor into a frying pan and lightly fry each floured joint, browning slightly on both sides. Remove and place in a pie dish. Then fry the onion in the hot Tomor for a few moments. Add to the rabbit along with the bacon and mushrooms. Season well with salt and pepper. Pour on the stock. Cover the pie dish with the pastry and bake at 220°C/425°F/Gas mark 7 for about 30 minutes. Remove from the oven. Cover the pastry with foil. Return to the oven, reduce the heat to 190°C/375°F/Gas mark 5 and cook for a further 30 minutes.

Cooking time: 1 hour.

BEEF CASSEROLE WITH MARJORAM

	Metric	Imperial	American
Flour	25 g	1 oz	1/4 cup
Salt	1/2 tsp	1/2 tsp	1/2 tsp
Pepper	1/4 tsp	1/4 tsp	1/4 tsp
Steak, cut into cubes	450 g	1 lb	1 lb
Tomor	25 g	1 oz	2 tbsp
Onions, chopped	2	2	2
Canned tomatoes	400 g	14 oz	14 oz
Chopped fresh or dried marjoram	1 tsp	1 tsp	1 tsp
Sugar	1/2 tsp	1/2 tsp	1/2 tsp

Rub the flour, salt and pepper into the meat. Heat the Tomor and fry the meat and onions in it. Remove from the pan and place in a casserole dish. Add the tomatoes, marjoram and sugar. Cover and cook at 150°C/300°F/Gas mark 2 for 1½–2 hours.

Cooking time: 1½–2 hours.

SHEPHERD'S PIE

	Metric	Imperial	American
Onions, chopped	2 large	2 large	2 large
Tomor	50 g	2 oz	1/4 cup
Minced beef	680 g	1½ lb	1½ lb
Flour	2 tbsp	2 tbsp	2 tbsp
Tomato purée	2 tbsp	2 tbsp	2 tbsp
Beef stock	150 ml	1/4 pt	2/3 cup
Salt and pepper			
Mashed potatoes	680 g	1½ lb	1½ lb

Cook the onions in half the Tomor until soft. Add the meat. Brown and drain off excess fat. Stir in the flour and mix until smooth. Add the tomato purée, stock, salt and pepper. Mix well and turn into an oven-proof dish. Cover with mashed potatoes and dot with Tomor. Bake uncovered at 180°C/350°F/Gas mark 4 for 35–45 minutes.

Cooking time: 35–45 minutes.

SAVOURY BACON ROLL

	Metric	Imperial	American
Tomor	15 g	½ oz	1 tbsp
Onion, finely chopped	1 small	1 small	1 small
Streaky bacon, finely chopped	225 g	8 oz	½ lb
Parsley, chopped	1 tbsp	1 tbsp	1 tbsp
Suet pastry (page 135)	225 g	8 oz	½ lb

Heat the oven. Heat the Tomor and gently fry the onion and bacon. Add the parsley. Remove from the pan. Make the pastry. Roll into an oblong and spread with the bacon and onion mixture, leaving about 1.25 cm/½ inch each side. Damp the edges with water and roll up tightly. Place on a Tomor-greased baking sheet and bake at 190°C/375°F/Gas mark 5 for about 1 hour.

Cooking time: 1 hour.

POTATO AND BACON PASTIES

	Metric	Imperial	American
Potato	100 g	4 oz	¼ lb
Onion	1 small	1 small	1 small
Lean bacon, chopped	225 g	8 oz	½ lb
Salt	1 tsp	1 tsp	1 tsp
Pepper	¼ tsp	¼ tsp	¼ tsp
Milk-free shortcrust **pastry (page 133)**	340 g	12 oz	¾ lb

Cut the potatoes and onion into very small pieces and add to the meat. Mix these together in a basin with the salt and pepper. Heat the oven. Divide the pastry into 4 and shape each portion into a ball. Roll out into a circle. Place a quarter of the filling on each circle, damp the edges with water and fold over. Press well and crimp. Prick the top with a fork. Bake at 220°C/425°F/Gas mark 7 for about 30 minutes.

Cooking time: 30 minutes.

SPAGHETTI BOLOGNESE

	Metric	Imperial	American
Tomor	15 g	½ oz	1 tbsp
Onion, chopped	1 large	1 large	1 large
Minced beef	225 g	8 oz	½ lb
Garlic, crushed	1 clove	1 clove	1 clove
Canned tomatoes	200 g	7 oz	7 oz
Tomato purée	3 tbsp	3 tbsp	3 tbsp
Pinch of mixed herbs			
Stock	150 ml	¼ pt	⅔ cup
Salt and pepper			
Egg-free spaghetti	225 g	8 oz	½ lb

Heat the Tomor in a saucepan, and fry the onion and meat slowly for 5 minutes. Then add the garlic, tomatoes, tomato purée, mixed herbs and stock. Season with salt and pepper. Cover and simmer gently for about 20–25 minutes. Cook the spaghetti as directed on the packet, drain and rinse. Serve the spaghetti with the sauce poured over.

Cooking time: 25 minutes.

CORNED BEEF AND PASTA SALAD

	Metric	Imperial	American
Egg-free pasta, small wheels	100 g	4 oz	¼ lb
Olive oil	4 tbsp	4 tbsp	4 tbsp
Lemon juice	1½ tbsp	1½ tbsp	1½ tbsp
Chilled corned beef	225 g	8 oz	½ lb
Canned sweetcorn with peppers	200 g	7 oz	7 oz
Celery, chopped	2 sticks	2 sticks	2 sticks
Cooked peas	100 g	4 oz	¼ lb
Salt and pepper			
Lettuce	1	1	1

Cook the pasta then drain well. Mix the oil and lemon juice together, pour over the pasta and stir gently. Allow the pasta to cool. Chop the corned beef into cubes. Drain the sweetcorn. When the pasta has cooled, add the sweetcorn, celery, peas and corned beef. Season with salt and pepper and mix.

Wash the lettuce and arrange around a salad bowl. Place the pasta mixture in the centre.

Cooking time: 20 minutes.

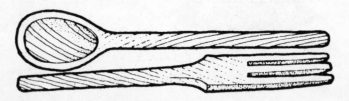

MACARONI BAKE

	Metric	Imperial	American
Tomor	25 g	1 oz	2 tbsp
Onions, finely chopped	100 g	4 oz	1 cup
Minced beef	450 g	1 lb	1 lb
Salt and pepper			
Cinnamon	½ tsp	½ tsp	½ tsp
Egg-free short-cut macaroni	225 g	8 oz	½ lb
Tomato juice	225 ml	8 fl oz	1 cup
Sliced tomatoes and watercress for garnish			

Melt the Tomor in a frying pan and fry the onion for a few minutes. Add the meat. Season with salt, pepper and cinnamon. Fry gently for 15 minutes, stirring frequently. Grease an oven-proof casserole dish with Tomor. Half cook the macaroni and place in the casserole. When the meat and onions are cooked, remove from the frying pan and add to the macaroni. Stir gently. Pour on the tomato juice. Heat the oven and bake at 180°C/350°F/Gas mark 4 for about 30 minutes. Add a little water if the mixture becomes too dry. Serve garnished with sliced tomatoes and watercress.

Cooking time: 45 minutes.

CORNISH PASTIES

	Metric	Imperial	American
Potato	100 g	4 oz	1/4 lb
Onion	1 small	1 small	1 small
Minced beef	225 g	8 oz	1/2 lb
Salt	1 tsp	1 tsp	1 tsp
Pepper	1/4 tsp	1/4 tsp	1/4 tsp
Milk-free shortcrust pastry (page 133)	340 g	12 oz	3/4 lb

Cut the potatoes and onion into very small pieces and add to the meat. Mix these together in a basin with the salt and pepper. Heat the oven. Divide the pastry in 4 and shape each portion into a ball. Roll out into a circle and place a quarter of the filling on each circle. Damp the edges with water and fold over. Press well and crimp. Prick the top with a fork. Bake at 220°C/425°F/Gas mark 7 for about 30 minutes.

Cooking time: 30 minutes.

MINTY LAMB CUTLETS

	Metric	Imperial	American
Lamb cutlets	8	8	8
Oil	1 tbsp	1 tbsp	1 tbsp
Tomor	25 g	1 oz	2 tbsp
Mint	1 tsp	1 tsp	1 tsp
Garlic (optional)	1/2 clove	1/2 clove	1/2 clove
Salt and pepper			
Lemon juice	1 tbsp	1 tbsp	1 tbsp

Trim the cutlets and place in a casserole. Heat the oil and Tomor in a pan. Add the mint, garlic, salt, pepper and lemon juice and stir. Remove from the heat and pour over the cutlets. Leave to marinate for about 1 hour.

Heat the grill. Remove the cutlets, drain and place under the grill. Cook for about 6 minutes each side, brushing occasionally with the marinade.

Cooking time: 12 minutes.

PORK FILLET WITH ORANGE SAUCE

	Metric	Imperial	American
Pork fillet	225 g	8 oz	½ lb
Tomor	15 g	½ oz	1 tbsp
Orange	1	1	1
Onion, chopped	1 small	1 small	1 small
Flour	1 tbsp	1 tbsp	1 tbsp
Redcurrant jelly	1 tbsp	1 tbsp	1 tbsp
Stock	150 ml	¼ pt	⅔ cup
Salt and pepper			

Slice the pork fillet thinly. Heat the Tomor and fry the meat slices until tender. Remove from the pan. Squeeze the juice from the orange. Fry the onion until soft, stir in the flour, orange juice, redcurrant jelly and stock. Bring to the boil. Return pork to the pan. Season well, simmer gently for a few minutes and serve.

Cooking time: 15 minutes.

HAMBURGERS

	Metric	Imperial	American
Minced beef	450 g	1 lb	1 lb
Onion, finely chopped	2 tbsp	2 tbsp	2 tbsp
Salt	1 tsp	1 tsp	1 tsp
Pepper	1 pinch	1 pinch	1 pinch
Tomor (if required)	15 g	½ oz	1 tbsp

Put the meat, onion and seasoning in a bowl and lightly mix together. Divide into 6–8 portions and form into flat rounds without pressing together too much. Fry in Tomor or grill to individual taste.

Cooking time: 15–20 minutes.

STUFFED BACON ROLLS

	Metric	Imperial	American
Sage and onion stuffing mix	225 g	8 oz	½ lb
Lean bacon	8 rashers	8 rashers	8 rashers
Water	2 tbsp	2 tbsp	2 tbsp

Mix the stuffing. Rind the bacon. Place a ball of stuffing on each bacon rasher and roll up. Secure with a wooden cocktail stick. Place in a shallow oven-proof dish. Pour in a small amount of water.

Cook at 180°C/350°F/Gas mark 4 for about 35 minutes.

Serve with mashed potatoes, peas or Brussels sprouts.

Cooking time: 35 minutes.

BACON AND SYRUP HOT POT

	Metric	Imperial	American
Thick streaky bacon (1 piece)	680 g	1½ lb	1½ lb
Onion	1 large	1 large	1 large
Celery	2 sticks	2 sticks	2 sticks
Canned butter beans	175 g	6 oz	6 oz
Mustard	½ tsp	½ tsp	½ tsp
Pepper	¼ tsp	¼ tsp	¼ tsp
Pure cane syrup	2 tbsp	2 tbsp	2 tbsp
Hot stock	600 ml	1 pt	2½ cups

Soak the bacon overnight in cold water. Drain and cut into four pieces. Place in an oven-proof dish. Peel and slice the onion. Wash and chop the celery. Add both to the casserole with the drained butter beans. Mix the mustard, pepper and syrup with a little of the stock. Pour over the bacon. Then pour on the rest of the stock, making sure it covers the bacon. Put on the lid and cook at 170°C/325°F/Gas mark 3 for 2 hours. Then remove the lid and cook for a further 1 hour to brown the meat.

Cooking time: 3 hours.

QUICK HERB PANCAKES

	Metric	Imperial	American
Suet	75 g	3 oz	¾ cup
Pinch of salt			
Plain flour	175 g	6 oz	1½ cups
Dried mixed herbs	1 tsp	1 tsp	1 tsp
Cold water	6–8 tbsp	6–8 tbsp	6–8 tbsp
Tomor			

Place the suet, salt, flour and herbs in a mixing bowl. Add the water and mix until the bowl is clean. Turn out onto a floured board and roll out thinly. Cut into rounds with a scone cutter. Place a knob of Tomor in a frying pan. Add the pancakes and fry until golden brown on both sides. Serve immediately sprinkled with salt.

Cooking time: 5–10 minutes.

Variation: To make **Lemon pancakes**, follow the recipe above, but omit the mixed herbs. When golden brown remove from the pan. Squeeze fresh lemon juice over them and sprinkle with sugar. Eat immediately.

SANDWICH SPREADS AND FILLINGS

Sandwich fillings never need to be boring. Experiment with a few appetising mixtures, such as the ones listed below, as well as trying the recipes.

Flaked salmon with finely chopped watercress.
Tuna and chopped celery.
Lamb with grated raw carrot.
Ham and pineapple.
Minced cooked liver with ham.
Corned beef and tomato.
Peanut butter with chopped onion and cress.
Marmite.
Banana and honey.

LIVER PÂTÉ

	Metric	Imperial	American
Tomor	50 g	2 oz	¼ cup
Streaky bacon	2 rashers	2 rashers	2 rashers
Onion, sliced	1	1	1
Liver, chopped	175 g	6 oz	6 oz
Salt and pepper			

Melt 25 g/1 oz of the Tomor in a frying pan. Fry the bacon and sliced onion, then remove from the pan. Next, fry the liver. Place the liver, onion, bacon and the remaining Tomor in the liquidiser. Season with salt and pepper. Blend until smooth.

HERRING ROE PÂTÉ

	Metric	Imperial	American
Tomor	50 g	2 oz	¼ cup
Soft herring roes	100 g	4 oz	¼ lb
Parsley, chopped	2 tbsp	2 tbsp	2 tbsp
Lemon juice	1 tbsp	1 tbsp	1 tbsp
Salt and pepper			

Melt 25 g/1 oz of the Tomor in a saucepan. Add the herring roes and fry gently for about 10 minutes. Soften the remaining Tomor without melting it. Mash or liquidise the roes. Add the Tomor, chopped parsley, lemon juice, salt and pepper. Mix well. Serve on toast or as a sandwich filling.

For babies, spread on thinly sliced bread or rusks.

Cooking time: 10 minutes.

SARDINE AND TOMATO SPREAD

	Metric	Imperial	American
Sardines	1–2	1–2	1–2
Tomato, skinned and deseeded (or 1 tbsp tomato ketchup)	1	1	1

Place sardines and tomato in a dish. Mash well with a fork. For babies, spread on thinly sliced bread or rusks.

CARROT AND PEANUT BUTTER SPREAD

	Metric	Imperial	American
Carrot, chopped	1	1	1
Peanut butter	1 tbsp	1 tbsp	1 tbsp

Place in the liquidiser and blend until smooth.

SAVOURY BEEF SPREAD

	Metric	Imperial	American
Cold cooked beef	2–3 slices	2–3 slices	2–3 slices
Shallots	1–2	1–2	1–2
Milk-free savoury white sauce (page 137)	2 tsp	2 tsp	2 tsp

Place in the liquidiser and blend until smooth.

HAM AND CHUTNEY SPREAD

	Metric	Imperial	American
Cold cooked ham	2 slices	2 slices	2 slices
Chutney	1–2 tsp	1–2 tsp	1–2 tsp

Place in the liquidiser and blend until smooth.

CAKES, SCONES AND TEABREADS

Most eggless cakes are better if eaten a day or two after baking.

YORKSHIRE PARKIN

	Metric	Imperial	American
Medium oatmeal	225 g	8 oz	2⅔ cups
Self-raising flour	100 g	4 oz	1 cup
Molasses sugar	100 g	4 oz	½ cup
Ground ginger	1½ tsp	1½ tsp	1½ tsp
Tomor	75 g	3 oz	⅓ cup
Golden syrup	250 g	9 oz	9 oz
Super creamy milk-free milk (page 146)	200 ml	7 fl oz	scant 1 cup

Line a 20 cm/8 inch square baking tin with greaseproof paper. Place all the dry ingredients in a mixing bowl. Melt the Tomor in a saucepan and add to the dry ingredients. Then add the syrup and super creamy milk-free milk. Mix well and pour the mixture into the baking tin. Bake at 170°C/325°F/Gas mark 3 for about 2 hours.

Cooking time: 2 hours.

FRESH ORANGE AND RAISIN LOAF

	Metric	Imperial	American
Self-raising flour	225 g	8 oz	2 cups
Bicarbonate of soda	½ tsp	½ tsp	½ tsp
Tomor	50 g	2 oz	¼ cup
Muscovado sugar	100 g	4 oz	½ cup
Seedless raisins	175 g	6 oz	1 cup
Juice and grated rind of ½ orange			
Basic soya milk (page 145)	120 ml	4 fl oz	½ cup

Line a ½ kg/1 lb loaf tin with greaseproof paper and brush with Tomor. Heat the oven. Sieve the flour and bicarbonate of soda into a mixing bowl, rub in the Tomor, add the sugar, raisins and grated orange rind. Mix well. Place the orange juice in a measuring jug and make up to 150 ml/ ¼ pt/⅔ cup with soya milk. Now stir the liquid into the dry ingredients and mix well until it forms a dropping consistency. Pour the mixture into the prepared tin and make a hollow in the centre. Bake at 180°C/350°F/Gas mark 4 for 20 minutes, then reduce the heat to 170°C/325°F/Gas mark 3 and bake for a further 1¼ hours.

Cooking time: 1½–1¾ hours.

HONEY MALT LOAF

	Metric	Imperial	American
Fresh yeast	25 g	1 oz	1 oz
Muscovado sugar	1 tsp	1 tsp	1 tsp
Warm water	150 ml	¼ pt	⅔ cup
Pure cane syrup	2 tbsp	2 tbsp	2 tbsp
Malt extract BP	4 tbsp	4 tbsp	4 tbsp
Tomor	25 g	1 oz	2 tbsp
Plain flour	450 g	1 lb	4 cups
Salt	½ tsp	½ tsp	½ tsp
Sultanas	100 g	4 oz	⅔ cup
Honey			

Grease two ½ kg/1 lb loaf tins with Tomor. Cream the yeast and sugar together, then add the warm water. Leave to stand for about 5 minutes until frothy. Melt the syrup, malt extract and Tomor in a saucepan over a low heat. Mix well. Remove from the heat and allow to cool. Sieve the flour and salt into a mixing bowl. Add the sultanas. Now pour the cooled malt mixture into the frothy yeast liquid. Make a well in the centre of the dry ingredients and add the malt and yeast mixture. Mix well to form a soft dough. Keep mixing until the bowl becomes clean. Turn out onto a lightly floured board and knead well until the dough becomes smooth and elastic. Divide the dough into two, then shape each piece to fit the prepared tins. Cover and leave to rise. Bake at 200°C/400°F/Gas mark 6 for about 45 minutes. While still hot, brush the loaves with honey.

Cooking time: 45 minutes.

Note: Use malt extract BP only. Virol contains egg.

GRANNY CAKE

	Metric	Imperial	American
Self-raising flour	225 g	8 oz	2 cups
Salt	½ tsp	½ tsp	½ tsp
Molasses sugar	25 g	1 oz	2 tbsp
Chopped walnuts	50 g	2 oz	⅓ cup
Raisins or sultanas	75 g	3 oz	½ cup
Pure cane syrup	1 tbsp	1 tbsp	1 tbsp
Super creamy milk-free milk (page 146)	150 ml	¼ pt	⅔ cup
Honey			

Heat the oven. Line a 15 cm/6 inch cake tin with greaseproof paper and brush with Tomor. Place the flour, salt and sugar in a mixing bowl and add the walnuts and fruit. Pour in the syrup and milk, and beat until very soft. Pour the mixture into the prepared tin. Bake at 180°C/350°F/Gas mark 4 for about 45 minutes. Brush the cake with honey while still hot.

Cooking time: 45 minutes.

SULTANA AND WALNUT TEA BREAD

	Metric	Imperial	American
100% wholemeal flour	175 g	6 oz	1½ cups
Self-raising flour	100 g	4 oz	1 cup
Baking powder	½ tsp	½ tsp	½ tsp
Nutmeg	¼ tsp	¼ tsp	¼ tsp
Sultanas	175 g	6 oz	1 cup
Chopped walnuts	50 g	2 oz	⅓ cup
Natural demerara sugar	100 g	4 oz	½ cup
Pure cane syrup	225 g	8 oz	1 cup
Basic soya milk (page 145)	150 ml	¼ pt	⅔ cup

Heat the oven. Line a 1 kg/2 lb loaf tin with greaseproof paper and brush lightly with Tomor. Sieve the wholemeal flour (putting the bran aside), self-raising flour, baking powder and nutmeg into a mixing bowl. Add the sultanas, chopped walnuts and sugar to the flour. Mix well.

Warm the syrup in a saucepan over a low heat. Add the soya milk and mix together until they combine. Remove from the heat. Stir into the dry ingredients. Mix well and turn the mixture into the prepared tin. Sprinkle on the bran from the flour. Bake at 180°C/350°F/Gas mark 4 for 1–1¼ hours. Leave to cool in the tin.

Serve spread with Tomor.

Cooking time: 1–1¼ hours.

SPICY TREACLE AND CINNAMON CAKE

	Metric	Imperial	American
100% wholemeal flour	225 g	8 oz	2 cups
Salt	½ tsp	½ tsp	½ tsp
Cinnamon	½ tsp	½ tsp	½ tsp
Mixed spice	1 heaped tsp	1 heaped tsp	1 heaped tsp
Bicarbonate of soda	⅓ tsp	⅓ tsp	⅓ tsp
Tomor	100 g	4 oz	½ cup
Molasses sugar	50 g	2 oz	¼ cup
Pure cane syrup	5 tbsp	5 tbsp	5 tbsp
Basic soya milk (page 145)	6 tbsp	6 tbsp	6 tbsp

Line a 15 cm/6 inch cake tin with greaseproof paper and brush with Tomor. Sieve the flour (reserving the bran), salt, cinnamon, mixed spice and bicarbonate of soda together in a mixing bowl. Rub in the Tomor. Add the sugar and stir. Put the syrup in a saucepan and warm slightly. Allow to cool a little, then pour into the mixture. Add the soya milk, stir thoroughly and beat well. Turn the mixture into the prepared tin and smooth the top. Sprinkle on the bran from the flour. Bake in the centre of the oven at 180°C/350°F/Gas mark 4 for 1¼–1½ hours.

Cooking time: 1¼ – 1½ hours.

CHOCOLATE FUDGE SLICE

	Metric	Imperial	American
Semolina shortbread biscuits (page 111)	225 g	8 oz	½ lb
Golden syrup	4 tbsp	4 tbsp	4 tbsp
Tomor	100 g	4 oz	½ cup
Drinking chocolate	2 tbsp	2 tbsp	2 tbsp
For the icing:			
Tomor	50 g	2 oz	¼ cup
Icing sugar	8 heaped tbsp	8 heaped tbsp	8 heaped tbsp
Super creamy milk-free milk (page 146)	2 tsp	2 tsp	2 tsp

Place the shortbread biscuits in a polythene bag and crush with a rolling pin. Melt the syrup and Tomor in a saucepan over a low heat. Remove from the heat, add the drinking chocolate and crushed biscuits. Mix well. Turn the mixture into a shallow 18 cm/7 inch cake tin and smooth the top.

For the icing, cream the Tomor and icing sugar together, then beat in the milk. Spread evenly over the fudge mixture. Mark into fingers with a fork. Leave to set.

Note: See page 9 on the use of coconut and cocoa products.

DATE BREAD

	Metric	Imperial	American
Plain flour	225 g	8 oz	2 cups
Baking powder	3 tsp	3 tsp	3 tsp
Salt	½ tsp	½ tsp	½ tsp
Bicarbonate of soda	⅛ tsp	⅛ tsp	⅛ tsp
Chopped dates	75 g	3 oz	½ cup
Chopped walnuts	40 g	1½ oz	¼ cup
Pure cane syrup	50 g	2 oz	4 tbsp
Tomor	25 g	1 oz	2 tbsp
Natural demerara sugar	50 g	2 oz	¼ cup
Basic soya milk (page 145)	150 ml	¼ pt	⅔ cup

Heat the oven. Line a 1 kg/2 lb loaf tin with greaseproof paper and brush with Tomor. Sieve the flour, baking powder, salt and bicarbonate of soda together in a mixing bowl. Add the chopped dates and walnuts. Melt the syrup, Tomor and sugar in a saucepan over a low heat. Add the soya milk but be careful not to boil. Pour the warm mixture over the dry ingredients. Mix thoroughly without beating to a stiff batter consistency. Pour into the prepared tin. Bake at 180°C/350°F/Gas mark 4 for about 1¼ hours.

Cooking time: 1¼ hours.

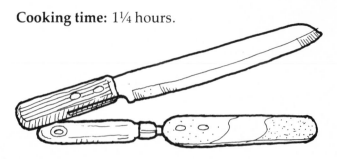

CHERRY FRUIT CAKE

	Metric	Imperial	American
Molasses sugar	175 g	6 oz	¾ cup
Chopped walnuts	250 g	9 oz	1½ cups
Chopped blanched almonds	75 g	3 oz	½ cup
Tomor	25 g	1 oz	2 tbsp
Cinnamon	1 tsp	1 tsp	1 tsp
Ground cloves	¼ tsp	¼ tsp	¼ tsp
Ground nutmeg	¼ tsp	¼ tsp	¼ tsp
Water	225 ml	8 fl oz	1 cup
Raisins	175 g	6 oz	1 cup
Mixed dried fruit	250 g	9 oz	1½ cups
Glacé cherries, halved	175 g	6 oz	1 cup
Bicarbonate of soda	1 tsp	1 tsp	1 tsp
Plain flour (white or wholemeal)	225 g	8 oz	2 cups
Baking powder	4 tsp	4 tsp	4 tsp
Salt	¼ tsp	¼ tsp	¼ tsp

Heat the oven. Line a 20 cm/8 inch round cake tin with greaseproof paper and brush lightly with melted Tomor. Put the sugar, nuts, Tomor, spices, water and fruit into a large saucepan. Bring to the boil and boil for about 4 minutes. Remove from heat and allow to cool. Dissolve the bicarbonate of soda in a little boiling water, then add it to the fruit mixture. Sieve in the flour, baking powder and salt, then gently fold in. Turn the mixture into the tin. Bake at 180°C/350°F/Gas mark 4 for about 1¼ hours.

Cooking time: 1¼ hours.

Note: This cake may be used as a birthday or Christmas cake when decorated with Eggless almond paste and Eggless fondant icing (page 153).

BRAN LOAF

	Metric	Imperial	American
All Bran	75 g	3 oz	1½ cups
Mixed fruit	225 g	8 oz	1⅓ cups
Muscovado sugar	225 g	8 oz	1 cup
Basic soya milk (page 145)	300 ml	½ pt	1¼ cups
Self-raising flour	175 g	6 oz	1½ cups
Baking powder	1 tsp	1 tsp	1 tsp

Put the All Bran, mixed fruit, sugar and soya milk into a basin, mix well and leave to soak for about 3–4 hours. Heat the oven. Line a 1 kg/2 lb loaf tin with greaseproof paper and brush with Tomor. Sieve the flour and baking powder into the mixture and stir well. Pour the mixture into the prepared tin. Bake in the centre of the oven at 190°C/375°F/Gas mark 5 for 1–1¼ hours.

Serve sliced and spread with Tomor.

Cooking time: 1–1¼ hours.

ICED FRUIT GINGERBREAD

	Metric	Imperial	American
Plain flour	175 g	6 oz	1½ cups
Salt	½ tsp	½ tsp	½ tsp
Ground ginger	1 tsp	1 tsp	1 tsp
Bicarbonate of soda	½ tsp	½ tsp	½ tsp
Sultanas	40 g	1½ oz	¼ cup
Preserved ginger	40 g	1½ oz	¼ cup
Candied peel	15 g	½ oz	1 tbsp
Tomor	50 g	2 oz	¼ cup
Molasses sugar	50 g	2 oz	¼ cup
Pure cane syrup	2 tbsp	2 tbsp	2 tbsp
Basic soya milk (page 145)	75 ml	2½ fl oz	⅓ cup
For the topping:			
Icing sugar	175 g	6 oz	1⅓ cups
Warm water	1–2 tbsp	1–2 tbsp	1–2 tbsp

Line a 15 cm/6 inch square tin with greaseproof paper and brush lightly with melted Tomor. Heat the oven. Sieve the flour, salt, ginger and bicarbonate of soda together. Add the sultanas, preserved ginger and candied peel. Mix well. Melt the Tomor, sugar and syrup in a saucepan over a low heat. Remove from the heat and add to the dry ingredients with the soya milk. Stir well, but do not beat. Pour into the prepared tin. Bake in the middle of the oven at 170°C/325°F/Gas mark 3 for about 1–1¼ hours.

To make the topping, sieve the icing sugar into a bowl and add the water a drop at a time until the icing is thick enough to coat the back of a spoon.

When the gingerbread is cool spread with glacé icing.

Cooking time: 1–1¼ hours.

WHOLEMEAL WELSH TREACLE CAKE

	Metric	Imperial	American
100% wholemeal flour	225 g	8 oz	2 cups
Tomor	70 g	2½ oz	5 tbsp
Mixed fruit	100 g	4 oz	⅔ cup
Molasses sugar	2 tbsp	2 tbsp	2 tbsp
Mixed spice	½ tsp	½ tsp	½ tsp
Basic soya milk (page 145)	2–3 tbsp	2–3 tbsp	2–3 tbsp
Pure cane syrup	1 tbsp	1 tbsp	1 tbsp

Heat the oven. Grease an oven-proof plate with Tomor. Put the flour into a mixing bowl and rub in the Tomor. Mix in the remaining dry ingredients and gradually add the syrup. Slowly mix in enough soya milk to make a fairly stiff consistency. Place the mixture on the oven-proof plate and bake at 190°C/375°F/Gas mark 5 for about 1 hour.

Cooking time: 1 hour.

RASPBERRY GATEAU

	Metric	Imperial	American
Self-raising flour	225 g	8 oz	2 cups
Tomor	50 g	2 oz	¼ cup
Caster sugar	50 g	2 oz	¼ cup
Super creamy milk-free milk (page 146)	1 tbsp	1 tbsp	1 tbsp
For the filling and decoration:			
Fresh raspberries	225 g	8 oz	½ lb
Milk free whipped cream (page 150)	150 ml	¼ pt	⅔ cup
Caster sugar			
Icing sugar			

Heat the oven. Grease two 23 cm/9 inch shallow cake tins with Tomor. Sieve the flour into a mixing bowl, rub in the Tomor. Add the sugar and mix to a fairly firm dough with the milk. Knead lightly, then divide into two equal portions. Form into rounds and place in the prepared tins. Bake at 220°C/425°F/Gas mark 7 for about 15 minutes until golden brown. Remove from the tins and allow to cool.

Reserve 8 raspberries for decoration. Then sandwich together with the fresh raspberries, sugar and whipped cream. Dust the top with icing sugar. Pipe 8 whirls of cream on top and place a raspberry on each whirl.

Cooking time: 15 minutes.

BOILED FRUIT CAKE

	Metric	Imperial	American
Self-raising flour	225 g	8 oz	2 cups
Nutmeg	½ tsp	½ tsp	½ tsp
Mixed spice	1 tsp	1 tsp	1 tsp
Salt	1 pinch	1 pinch	1 pinch
Tomor	100 g	4 oz	½ cup
Mixed fruit	225 g	8 oz	1⅓ cups
Molasses sugar	100 g	4 oz	½ cup
Hot water	12 tbsp	12 tbsp	12 tbsp
Bicarbonate of soda	½ tsp	½ tsp	½ tsp

Heat the oven. Line a 15 cm/6 inch cake tin with greaseproof paper. Sieve the flour, nutmeg, mixed spice and salt together in a mixing bowl. Put the Tomor, mixed fruit, sugar and hot water into a saucepan. Heat slowly until the Tomor has melted and the sugar dissolved, then bring to the boil. Reduce the heat again and allow to simmer for 2 minutes. Remove from the heat and cool until lukewarm. When cool add the bicarbonate of soda. Stir in quickly. Make a well in the centre of the dry ingredients and pour in the cooled mixture, stirring together quickly. Mix thoroughly. Pour the mixture into the prepared tin and smooth the top. Bake at 180°C/350°F/Gas mark 4 for 1¼ hours. When cooked remove the cake from the oven and leave in the tin for 5 minutes, then turn out and cool on a wire tray.

Cooking time: 1¼ hours.

HERB AND POTATO SCONES

	Metric	Imperial	American
Plain flour	100 g	4 oz	1 cup
Sieved cooked potatoes	100 g	4 oz	¼ lb
Baking powder	4 tsp	4 tsp	4 tsp
Salt	½ tsp	½ tsp	½ tsp
Mixed herbs	½–1 tsp	½–1 tsp	½–1 tsp
Tomor	40 g	1½ oz	3 tbsp
Super creamy milk-free milk (page 146)	75 ml	2½ fl oz	⅓ cup

Grease a baking tray with Tomor. Heat the oven. Sieve the flour, potatoes, baking powder and salt into a mixing bowl. Add the mixed herbs. Rub in the Tomor. Add the milk all at once and mix with a knife until a dough is formed. Turn out onto a floured board. Roll out until 2 cm/¾ inch thick. Cut into rounds with a scone cutter. Place on the prepared baking tray. Bake on the second shelf from the top at 230°C/450°F/Gas mark 8 for about 10 minutes.

Cooking time: 10 minutes.

SULTANA AND APPLE SCONES

	Metric	Imperial	American
Plain flour	225 g	8 oz	2 cups
Baking powder	4 tsp	4 tsp	4 tsp
Salt	½ tsp	½ tsp	½ tsp
Mixed spice	½ tsp	½ tsp	½ tsp
Tomor	40 g	1½ oz	3 tbsp
Sultanas	25 g	1 oz	3 tbsp
Molasses sugar	25 g	1 oz	2 tbsp
Apple, peeled and grated	1	1	1
Super creamy milk-free milk (page 146)	75 ml	2½ fl oz	⅓ cup
Natural demerara sugar			

Heat the oven. Grease a baking tray. Sieve the flour, baking powder, salt and mixed spice into a mixing bowl. Rub in the Tomor. Add the sultanas, sugar and grated apple. Mix well. Then add the milk and mix to a soft dough. Roll out on a floured board until 2 cm/¾ inch thick. Cut into rounds with a scone cutter and place on the prepared baking tray. Brush with water then sprinkle with natural demerara sugar. Bake on the second shelf from the top at 230°C/450°F/Gas mark 8 for about 10 minutes.

Cooking time: 10 minutes.

SINGIN' HINNY

	Metric	Imperial	American
Plain flour	225 g	8 oz	2 cups
Baking powder	2 tsp	2 tsp	2 tsp
Salt	½ tsp	½ tsp	½ tsp
Lard or white vegetable fat	50 g	2 oz	¼ cup
Currants	50 g	2 oz	⅓ cup
Super creamy milk-free milk (page 146)	4 tbsp	4 tbsp	4 tbsp
Tomor	15 g	½ oz	1 tbsp
Caster sugar			

Sieve the flour, baking powder and salt into a mixing bowl. Rub in the white fat until it resembles fine breadcrumbs. Add the currants, and enough milk to form a soft (not sticky) dough. Place on a floured board and knead lightly. Roll out until 1.25 cm/½ inch thick. Brush a frying pan with a little melted Tomor. Heat gently. Place the dough in the frying pan and cook slowly for about 10–15 minutes, turning once. Cook until golden brown. Remove from the pan and sprinkle with caster sugar.

Serve hot, spread with Tomor.

Cooking time: 10–15 minutes.

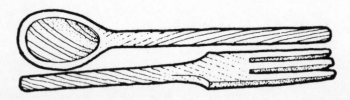

CREAM SPLITS

	Metric	Imperial	American
Plain flour	450 g	1 lb	4 cups
Salt	½ tsp	½ tsp	½ tsp
Yeast	15 g	½ oz	½ oz
Caster sugar	1 tsp	1 tsp	1 tsp
Super creamy milk-free milk (page 146) or milk and water	300 ml	½ pt	1¼ cups
Tomor	50 g	2 oz	¼ cup
For the filling:			
Jam			
Milk-free whipped cream (page 150)	150 ml	¼ pt	⅔ cup
Icing sugar			

Grease and flour two baking trays. Sieve the flour and salt into a mixing bowl. Cream the yeast with the sugar. Put the super creamy milk into a saucepan and warm to blood heat. Then melt the Tomor in the milk. Make a well in the centre of the dry ingredients and pour the yeast, milk and melted Tomor in at once. Mix to a soft dough. Flour another bowl and put the mixture into it, cover with a damp cloth and leave to rise in a warm place until it has doubled in size. Turn out the dough and divide into 16 equal portions. Knead into small balls and place on the prepared baking trays – leave to prove for 15–20 minutes. Heat the oven. When the buns have risen, bake at 230°C/450°F/Gas mark 8 for 15–20 minutes.

When cool, split the buns and fill with milk-free whipped cream and jam. Dust with a little icing sugar.

Cooking time: 15–20 minutes.

BISCUITS AND COOKIES

Home made biscuits are delicious and well worth the time and effort spent in making them. They keep almost indefinitely if stored in an airtight tin or jar, away from cakes and bread.

OAT CRISPIES

	Metric	Imperial	American
Self-raising flour	50 g	2 oz	½ cup
Rolled oats	225 g	8 oz	2½ cups
Salt	¼ tsp	¼ tsp	¼ tsp
Bicarbonate of soda	¼ tsp	¼ tsp	¼ tsp
Tomor	100 g	4 oz	½ cup
Pure cane syrup	4 tbsp	4 tbsp	4 tbsp
Muscovado sugar	50–75 g	2–3 oz	4–6 tbsp

Heat the oven. Grease a Swiss roll tin with Tomor. Mix the flour, oats, salt and bicarbonate of soda together in a basin. Melt the Tomor, syrup and the sugar in a large saucepan over a low heat. Cool, then add the dry ingredients and mix thoroughly. Remove from the saucepan and press firmly into the prepared tin. Bake at 180°C/350°F/ Gas mark 4 for about 45–50 minutes. Cut into rectangles while still warm.

Cooking time: 45–50 minutes.

TWINKLING STARS

	Metric	Imperial	American
Self-raising flour	225 g	8 oz	2 cups
Ground rice	100 g	4 oz	1 cup
Caster sugar	175 g	6 oz	¾ cup
Tomor	175 g	6 oz	¾ cup
Lemon essence	¼ tsp	¼ tsp	¼ tsp
Super creamy milk-free milk (page 146)	4 tbsp	4 tbsp	4 tbsp
For the decoration:			
Icing sugar	175 g	6 oz	1⅓ cups
Warm water	1–2 tbsp	1–2 tbsp	1–2 tbsp
Silver dragees			

Heat the oven. Grease two baking trays with Tomor. Place the flour, ground rice and sugar in a mixing bowl and mix thoroughly. Rub in the Tomor. Add the lemon essence and milk. Mix to a stiff dough. Roll out thinly on a floured board and cut into stars with a cutter. Place on the prepared trays. Bake at 170°C/325°F/Gas mark 3 for about 15 minutes.

To make the icing, sieve the icing sugar into a bowl and mix in the water a drop at a time until the icing is thick enough to coat the back of a spoon. When cool, cover the top of each biscuit with the glacé icing and place a silver dragee on each point.

Cooking time: 15 minutes.

SAVOURY SOYA BISCUITS

	Metric	Imperial	American
100% wholemeal flour	100 g	4 oz	1 cup
Baking powder	1 tsp	1 tsp	1 tsp
Basic soya milk (page 145)	70 ml	2¼ fl oz	scant ⅓ cup
Tomor	15 g	½ oz	1 tbsp

Lightly grease a baking tray with Tomor. Heat the oven. Sieve the flour and baking powder together. Put the soya milk in a saucepan and warm slightly. Melt the Tomor in the milk. Add the liquid to the dry ingredients. Mix well. Turn out onto a floured board and roll out very thinly. Cut into rounds with a scone cutter and prick with a fork. Bake at 180°C/350°F/Gas mark 4 for about 15 minutes.

Cooking time: 15 minutes.

Note: Serve spread with a milk-free herb butter (pages 151-2).

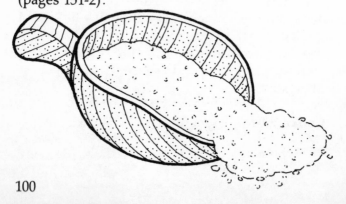

GINGERBREAD MEN

	Metric	Imperial	American
Tomor	100 g	4 oz	½ cup
Muscovado sugar	100 g	4 oz	½ cup
Plain flour	275 g	10 oz	2½ cups
Bicarbonate of soda	1 tsp	1 tsp	1 tsp
Ground ginger	3 tsp	3 tsp	3 tsp
Pure cane syrup	2½ tbsp	2½ tbsp	2½ tbsp
Currants			

Heat the oven. Grease a baking tray with Tomor. Cream the Tomor and sugar until very soft. Sieve the dry ingredients together, then work into the creamed mixture. Add the syrup to make a dough. Knead and roll out on a floured board. Cut out, using a special cutter if available, or a cardboard pattern and a sharp-pointed knife. Place the figures on the baking tray and add the currants to represent eyes and buttons. Bake for about 15 minutes at 190°C/375°F/Gas mark 5 and allow to cool before removing from the baking tray.

Cooking time: 15 minutes.

Variation: At Easter make Easter bunnies instead.

HIGH-FIBRE SHORTCAKE FINGERS

	Metric	Imperial	American
Tomor	100 g	4 oz	½ cup
Desiccated coconut	100 g	4 oz	1⅓ cups
Rolled oats	100 g	4 oz	1⅓ cups
Light muscovado sugar	50 g	2 oz	¼ cup
Vanilla essence	1 tsp	1 tsp	1 tsp
Baking powder	1 tsp	1 tsp	1 tsp
Pinch of salt			

Heat the oven. Grease a shallow 20 cm/8 inch square cake tin with Tomor. Melt the Tomor in a saucepan. Place all the other ingredients in a mixing bowl. Pour the melted Tomor onto the dry ingredients and mix well. Turn the mixture into the prepared tin and press down. Bake at 150°C/300°F/Gas mark 2 for about 45 minutes. When cold cut into fingers.

Cooking time: 45 minutes.

Note: See page 9 on the use of coconut and cocoa products.

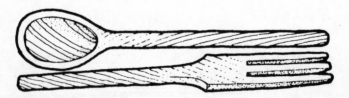

CHOCOLATE CRUNCHIES

	Metric	Imperial	American
Tomor	225 g	8 oz	1 cup
Muscovado sugar	150 g	5 oz	⅝ cup
Cocoa	1 tbsp	1 tbsp	1 tbsp
Desiccated coconut	75 g	3 oz	1 cup
Crushed cornflakes	65 g	2½ oz	⅝ cup
Self-raising flour	150 g	5 oz	1¼ cups

For decoration:

Terry's Bitter Bar (or Home-made milk-free chocolate, page 155)	225 g	8 oz	½ lb

Grease a Swiss roll tin with Tomor. Put the Tomor into a large saucepan and melt over a low heat. Remove from the heat and stir in the sugar, cocoa, coconut and cornflakes. Add the flour gradually and mix thoroughly. Turn into the prepared tin and smooth the top with a knife. Bake at 180°C/350°F/Gas mark 4 for about 30 minutes. Cut into rectangles while still warm.

When cold, cover with melted Terry's Bitter Bar or home-made milk-free chocolate.

Cooking time: 30 minutes.

Note: See page 9 on the use of coconut and cocoa products.

103

ICED ANIMAL BISCUITS

	Metric	Imperial	American
Icing sugar	100 g	4 oz	¾ cup
Tomor	100 g	4 oz	½ cup
Plain flour	225 g	8 oz	2 cups
Cornflour	100 g	4 oz	1⅓ cups
Basic soya milk (page 145)	4 tbsp	4 tbsp	4 tbsp
Vanilla essence	2 tsp	2 tsp	2 tsp
For the decoration:			
Icing sugar	175 g	6 oz	1⅓ cups
Warm water	1–2 tbsp	1–2 tbsp	1–2 tbsp
Food colouring			

Sieve the icing sugar into a mixing bowl. Add the Tomor and cream together until light and fluffy. Sieve the flour and cornflour into the creamed mixture and mix well. Add the soya milk and vanilla essence. Knead to form a soft dough. Remove from the bowl and leave in a cool place for about half an hour. Heat the oven. Grease a baking tray with Tomor. Place the dough on a floured board and roll out until 6 mm/¼ inch thick. Cut into shapes with an animal cutter. Bake at 200°C/400°F/Gas mark 6 for just over 10 minutes.

To make the icing, sieve the icing sugar into a bowl and add the water a drop at a time until the icing is thick enough to coat the back of a spoon. When the biscuits are cool decorate with glacé icing, coloured with a few drops of food colouring.

Cooking time: 10 minutes.

CHERRY FLAPJACKS

	Metric	Imperial	American
Tomor	100 g	4 oz	½ cup
Pure cane syrup	1 tsp	1 tsp	1 tsp
Self-raising flour	50 g	2 oz	½ cup
Muscovado sugar	100 g	4 oz	½ cup
Oats	50 g	2 oz	⅔ cup
Crushed cornflakes	75 g	3 oz	¾ cup
Glacé cherries, halved	100 g	4 oz	⅔ cup

Grease a Swiss roll tin with Tomor. Heat the oven. Melt the Tomor in a saucepan over a low heat. Stir in the syrup. (Do not boil.) Place the flour, sugar, oats and cornflakes in a mixing bowl and mix well. Pour the melted Tomor and syrup onto the dry ingredients and mix thoroughly. Place in the prepared tin and top with glacé cherries. Bake at 190°C/375°F/Gas mark 5 for 15–20 minutes. Remove from the oven and cut into fingers while still hot.

Cooking time: 15–20 minutes.

TRADITIONAL GINGER NUTS

	Metric	Imperial	American
Self-raising flour	100 g	4 oz	1 cup
Bicarbonate of soda	½ tsp	½ tsp	½ tsp
Ground ginger	2 tsp	2 tsp	2 tsp
Natural demerara sugar	2 tsp	2 tsp	2 tsp
Tomor	50 g	2 oz	¼ cup
Golden syrup	75 g	3 oz	6 tbsp

Heat the oven. Grease two baking trays. Sieve the flour, bicarbonate of soda, ginger and sugar together in a mixing bowl. Melt the Tomor in a saucepan over a low heat. Stir in the syrup. Remove from the heat and add to the dry ingredients. Stir well. Roll the mixture into small balls, then flatten a little. Place well apart on the prepared baking trays and bake at 190°C/375°F/Gas mark 5 for about 15–20 minutes. Cool before removing from the trays.

Cooking time: 15–20 minutes.

DIGESTIVE BISCUITS

	Metric	Imperial	American
Self-raising flour	150 g	5 oz	1¼ cups
Medium oatmeal	75 g	3 oz	1 cup
Salt	¼ tsp	¼ tsp	¼ tsp
Tomor	100 g	4 oz	½ cup
Caster sugar	1–2 tbsp	1–2 tbsp	1–2 tbsp
Basic soya milk (page 145)	1–2 tbsp	1–2 tbsp	1–2 tbsp

Grease a baking tray with Tomor. Heat the oven. Sieve the flour, oatmeal and salt into a mixing bowl and rub in the Tomor. Add the sugar and just enough liquid to bind. Roll out to less than 6 mm/¼ inch thick. Cut into rounds and prick with a fork. Bake at 180°C/350°F/Gas mark 4 until pale golden brown.

Cooking time: about 15 minutes.

HONEY BOURBON CREAMS

	Metric	Imperial	American
Tomor	50 g	2 oz	1/4 cup
Light muscovado sugar	50 g	2 oz	1/4 cup
Honey	1 tbsp	1 tbsp	1 tbsp
Plain flour	100 g	4 oz	1 cup
Cocoa	2 tbsp	2 tbsp	2 tbsp
Bicarbonate of soda	1/2 tsp	1/2 tsp	1/2 tsp
For the filling:			
Tomor	40 g	1 1/2 oz	3 tbsp
Icing sugar	75 g	3 oz	1 cup
Coffee essence	1 tsp	1 tsp	1 tsp
Cocoa	1 tbsp	1 tbsp	1 tbsp

Grease a baking tray with Tomor. Heat the oven. Cream the Tomor and sugar together. Add the honey. Sieve the flour, cocoa and bicarbonate of soda into the cream mixture. Stir and form into a firm dough. Knead well. Roll out to 3 mm/1/8 inch thick. Cut into fingers 6.5 cm × 1.5 cm/2½ × ¾ inch thick. Place on the prepared baking tray. Prick all over with a fork. Bake at 170°C/325°F/Gas mark 3 for 15–20 minutes. Remove from the oven. Place the biscuits on a wire tray and allow to cool.

To make the filling, cream the Tomor and icing sugar together until smooth. Add the coffee essence and cocoa and mix until creamy. Sandwich the fingers together with the filling.

Cooking time: 15–20 minutes.

Note: See page 9 on the use of coconut and cocoa products.

OATMEAL SQUARES

	Metric	Imperial	American
Tomor	100 g	4 oz	½ cup
Molasses sugar	50 g	2 oz	¼ cup
100% wholemeal flour	100 g	4 oz	1 cup
Salt	¼ tsp	¼ tsp	¼ tsp
Fine oatmeal	100 g	4 oz	1 cup
Super creamy milk-free milk (page 146)	60 ml	2 fl oz	¼ cup
Almonds, blanched and chopped	50 g	2 oz	½ cup

Heat the oven. Grease a Swiss roll tin with Tomor. Cream the Tomor and sugar together. Sieve in the flour, salt and oatmeal. Add the milk and mix to a firm dough. Place in the prepared tin and press down firmly. Sprinkle on the chopped almonds. Bake at 180°C/350°F/Gas mark 4 for about 20–25 minutes. When cool, cut into squares.

Cooking time: 20–25 minutes.

CHOCOLATE, HONEY AND HAZELNUT BISCUITS

	Metric	Imperial	American
Tomor	100 g	4 oz	1/2 cup
Caster sugar	65 g	2 1/2 oz	1/3 cup
Plain flour	150 g	5 oz	1 1/4 cups
Ground hazelnuts	75 g	3 oz	3/4 cup
For the filling and decoration:			
Honey			
Terry's Bitter Bar or Home-made milk-free chocolate page 155)	75 g	3 oz	1/4 cup
Ground hazelnuts	40 g	1 1/2 oz	3/8 cup

Heat the oven. Grease two baking trays with Tomor. Cream the Tomor and sugar together. Sieve the flour into the cream mixture. Add the ground hazelnuts. Knead, then turn out onto a floured board. Roll out thinly between two pieces of greaseproof paper. Cut into rounds with a scone cutter and place on the prepared baking trays. Bake at 180°C/350°F/Gas mark 4 for about 12 minutes. Allow to cool before removing from the trays.

Sandwich the biscuits together with honey. Melt the chocolate in a saucepan over hot water. Mix until smooth. Roll the edges of each biscuit in the melted chocolate and then in chopped nuts.

Cooking time: 12 minutes.

Note: See page 9 on the use of coconut and cocoa products.

SEMOLINA SHORTBREAD BISCUITS

	Metric	Imperial	American
Tomor	*100 g*	*4 oz*	*½ cup*
Self-raising flour	*100 g*	*4 oz*	*1 cup*
Fine semolina	*100 g*	*4 oz*	*1 cup*
Caster sugar	*50 g*	*2 oz*	*¼ cup*
Pinch of salt			

Heat the oven. Grease a baking tray with Tomor. Cream the Tomor. Mix the dry ingredients together and gradually add them to the Tomor. Mix well, then turn out onto a floured board and knead into one piece. Roll out thinly between two pieces of greaseproof paper. Cut into rounds with a scone cutter and place on the prepared baking tray. Bake at 170°C/325°F/Gas mark 3, for about 20 minutes. Sprinkle with caster sugar.

Cooking time: 20 minutes.

SOYA CRUNCH

	Metric	Imperial	American
Tomor	100 g	4 oz	¼ cup
Granulated sugar	475 g	1½ lb	3 cups
Basic soya milk (page 145)	300 ml	½ pt	1¼ cups

Melt the Tomor in a saucepan. Add the sugar and soya milk. Cook over a low heat until the sugar has dissolved. Then bring to the boil and boil gently for about 20 minutes, stirring occasionally until the mixture begins to darken and thicken. Remove from the heat and beat with a wooden spoon until the mixture begins to cool and thicken. Pour into a Tomor-greased Swiss roll tin. Cut into 2.5 cm/1 inch squares, using an oiled knife, before it is quite set.

Cooking time: 20 minutes.

Note: Children love these little sweets.

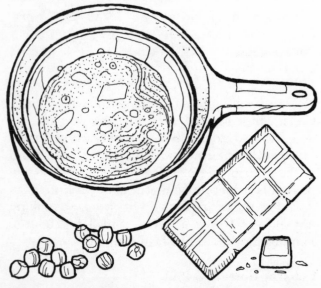

DESSERTS AND ICE-CREAM

PEARS IN CARAMEL CREAM

	Metric	Imperial	American
Sugar	175 g	6 oz	¾ cup
Cold water	100 ml	3½ fl oz	⅜ cup
Hot water	200 ml	⅓ pt	⅞ cup
Milk-free whipped cream (page 150) chilled	300 ml	½ pt	1¼ cups
Canned pear halves	400 g	14 oz	14 oz

Lightly oil a baking tray. Put the sugar and cold water into a saucepan and boil slowly to a good rich brown. Now pour a little of the caramel mixture onto the prepared baking tray. When cool, crush. Add the hot water to the remaining caramel mixture. Bring back to the boil. Remove from the heat and cool. Gently whip the milk-free cream and add the caramel mixture a little at a time. Whip until thick. Drain the pears. Either place alternate layers of sliced pears and cream in a large glass dish or individual dishes; or put the cream in individual dishes and place a pear half on top. Chill and top with the crushed caramel.

Note: Serve immediately.

RHUBARB AND HONEY CRUNCH

	Metric	Imperial	American
Rhubarb	450 g	1 lb	1 lb
Clear honey	1 tbsp	1 tbsp	1 tbsp
Water	1 tbsp	1 tbsp	1 tbsp
Plain flour	100 g	4 oz	1 cup
Tomor	65 g	2½ oz	5 tbsp
Natural demerara sugar	75 g	3 oz	⅜ cup
White breadcrumbs	50 g	2 oz	½ cup

Wash the rhubarb and cut into 2cm/1 inch pieces. Place in an oven-proof dish. Add the honey and water. Put the flour in a mixing bowl. Rub in the Tomor until the mixture resembles fine breadcrumbs. Add the sugar and breadcrumbs, mix thoroughly, and spread evenly over the fruit. Dot with Tomor. Bake at 180°C/375°F/Gas mark 4 for about 1 hour.

Cooking time: 1 hour.

TREACLE WHEEL

	Metric	Imperial	American
Milk-free shortcrust pastry (page 133)	175 g	6 oz	6 oz
Golden syrup	100 g	4 oz	½ cup
Fresh breadcrumbs	50 g	2 oz	½ cup
Lemon juice	1 tsp	1 tsp	1 tsp

Roll out the pastry and line a 18–20 cm/7–8 inch oven-proof plate. Warm the syrup in a saucepan, add the breadcrumbs and lemon juice. Remove from the heat and spread evenly over the pastry. Re-roll the pastry trimmings, cut into narrow strips and arrange like the spokes of a wheel, damping the ends so they stick in position. Bake at 190°C/375°F/Gas mark 5 for about 30 minutes.

Cooking time: 30 minutes.

CRANBERRY AND BANANA PIE

	Metric	Imperial	American
Tomor	40 g	1½ oz	3 tbsp
Fresh or frozen cranberries	275 g	10 oz	2½ cups
Muscovado sugar	50 g	2 oz	¼ cup
Cold water	350 ml	12 fl oz	1½ cups
Bananas	6	6	6
Sweet milk-free shortcrust pastry (page 134)	100 g	4 oz	4 oz

Heat the oven. Well grease a deep pie dish with Tomor. Wash the cranberries and place in a saucepan with the sugar and water. Cover and cook until the cranberries stop popping. Thinly slice the bananas. Place alternate layers of cranberries and bananas in the prepared pie dish. Roll out the pastry 1.5 cm/¾ inch thick. Cover the fruit with the pastry. Press the edges firmly onto the pie dish. Make three slits in the top. Bake at 220°C/425°F/Gas mark 7 for 15 minutes. Then reduce the heat to 180°C/350°F/Gas mark 4 for a further 15 minutes.

Cooking time: 30 minutes.

Note: This is an excellent dessert to follow poultry or game.

BLACKBERRY ROLY POLY

	Metric	Imperial	American
Self-raising flour	225 g	8 oz	2 cups
Pinch of salt			
Tomor	75 g	3 oz	1/3 cup
Caster sugar	25 g	1 oz	4 tbsp
Super creamy milk-free milk (page 146)	4 tbsp	4 tbsp	4 tbsp
For the filling:			
Fresh blackberries	350 g	12 oz	12 oz
Caster sugar	75 g	3 oz	3/8 cup
For the topping:			
Caster sugar	2 tsp	2 tsp	2 tsp
Tomor	25 g	1 oz	2 tbsp
Water	3 tbsp	3 tbsp	3 tbsp

Heat the oven. Sieve the flour and salt into a mixing bowl. Rub in the Tomor. Add the sugar and mix to a soft dough with the milk. Roll out the pastry to 30 × 25 cm (12 × 10 inch). Cover with the blackberries. Sprinkle with the sugar. Wet the edges of the pastry with water. Roll up like a Swiss roll. Seal firmly. Place in an oven-proof dish. Make three slits in the top. Sprinkle with the caster sugar, dot with Tomor. Pour the water into the dish. Bake at 220°C/425°F/Gas mark 7 for 15 minutes. Then reduce the heat to 190°C/375°F/Gas mark 5 and continue cooking for a further 25–30 minutes.

Cooking time: 45 minutes.

CREAMY HONEY BLANCMANGE BUNNIES

	Metric	Imperial	American
Cornflour	4 tbsp	4 tbsp	4 tbsp
Super creamy milk-free milk (page 146)	600 ml	1 pint	2½ cups
Honey	3 tbsp	3 tbsp	3 tbsp
Flavouring of your choice (see below for suggestions)			

Put the cornflour in a basin. Mix smoothly with a little super creamy milk. Put the rest of the milk on to heat. When nearly boiling gradually stir into the mixed cornflour. Stir well. Return the mixture to the pan and bring to the boil, stirring continuously. Then lower the heat. Add the honey, simmer gently, stirring constantly for 2–3 minutes until thick. Remove from heat. Add the desired flavouring. Stir until evenly blended. Pour into a wet rabbit mould. Chill.

Decorate if you wish with chilled Milk-free whipped cream (page 150).

Cooking time: 5–10 minutes.

Variations: For **Chocolate honey blancmange**, add 75 g/3 oz/1 cup of drinking chocolate.
For **Coffee honey blancmange**, add 1 tablespoon of instant coffee powder.

For **Lemon honey blancmange**, add the juice of 1 lemon and the finely grated rind of two lemons.

Note: See page 9 on the use of coconut and cocoa products.

RASPBERRY SURPRISE

	Metric	Imperial	American
Raspberry jelly	½ pkt	½ pkt	½ pkt
Water	150 ml	¼ pt	⅔ cup
Canned raspberries	225 g	8 oz	8 oz
Caster sugar	25 g	1 oz	4 tbsp
For the decoration:			
Milk-free whipped cream (page 150)	150 ml	¼ pt	⅔ cup
Glacé cherries			

Make the jelly by using water and juice from the can, made up to 300 ml/½ pt of liquid. Add the sugar and leave to cool. Then place in the refrigerator until the mixture begins to thicken. Remove and whisk until the mixture is spongy. Stir in the fruit. Pour into glasses. Return to the refrigerator to set, then decorate with milk-free whipped cream and cherries.

CARROT PLUM PUDDING

	Metric	Imperial	American
Raisins	175 g	6 oz	1 cup
Currants	150 g	5 oz	1 cup
Plain flour	100 g	4 oz	1 cup
Salt	½ tsp	½ tsp	½ tsp
Ground cinnamon	½ tsp	½ tsp	½ tsp
Grated nutmeg	½ tsp	½ tsp	½ tsp
Pinch of ground cloves			
Molasses sugar	225 g	8 oz	1 cup
Breadcrumbs, white or wholemeal	50 g	2 oz	½ cup
Shredded suet	100 g	4 oz	1 cup
Grated carrot	175 g	6 oz	1 cup
Grated raw potatoes	175 g	6 oz	1 cup
Juice of ½ lemon			
Chopped mixed peel	150 g	5 oz	1 cup
Bicarbonate of soda	1 tsp	1 tsp	1 tsp
A little warm water			

Grease a pudding basin. Clean the fruit. Sieve the flour, salt and spices together. Add the fruit, sugar, breadcrumbs, suet, carrots, potatoes, lemon juice, mixed peel and finally the bicarbonate of soda dissolved in a little warm water. (Add just enough to mix without making the mixture too wet.) Put in the greased pudding basin, filling it two-thirds full. Cover tightly and steam for about 3 hours.

Serve with Milk-free sweet white sauce (page 142).

Cooking time: 3 hours.

Note: This makes an excellent substitute for Christmas pudding.

BASIC APPLE DUMPLINGS

	Metric	Imperial	American
Medium apples	4	4	4
Sweet milk-free shortcrust pastry (page 134)	225 g	8 oz	8 oz
Natural demerara sugar	75 g	3 oz	1/3 cup

Heat the oven. Grease a baking tray with Tomor. Peel and core the apples. Divide the pastry into four and roll out into circles. Stand an apple in the centre of each pastry circle and fill the holes with sugar. Draw the pastry up and carefully mould it to completely cover the apple. Seal the edges. Place each apple dumpling on the prepared tray, with the sealed edges underneath. Bake at 180°C/350°F/Gas mark 4 for about 40 minutes until the apple is tender. Remove from the oven. Dredge with natural demerara sugar.

Cooking time: 40 minutes.

Variations: For **Spiced apple dumplings**, fill the apple centres with natural demerara sugar, chopped crystallised ginger and chopped walnuts.
For **Fruity apple dumplings**, fill the apple centres with a few raisins, chopped dates or figs.

SPICY LEMON AND APPLE STRUDEL

	Metric	Imperial	American
Sweet milk-free shortcrust pastry (page 134)	175 g	6 oz	6 oz
Cooking apples	450 g	1 lb	1 lb
Juice of 1 lemon			
Muscovado sugar	25 g	1 oz	4 tbsp
Cinnamon	1/4 tsp	1/4 tsp	1/4 tsp
Nutmeg	1/4 tsp	1/4 tsp	1/4 tsp
For the topping:			
Plain flour	75 g	3 oz	3/4 cup
Natural demerara sugar	75 g	3 oz	1/3 cup
Tomor (coarsely grated)	75 g	3 oz	1/3 cup
Grated rind of 1 lemon			

Heat the oven. Roll out the pastry and line a 18–20 cm/7–8 inch flan tin. Peel, core and slice the apples and squeeze lemon juice over them. Place the apple slices in the pastry case. Sprinkle with sugar and spices.

For the topping, put the flour, sugar, grated Tomor and lemon rind into a mixing bowl. Mix together until crumbly. Sprinkle over the sliced apples. Base at 230°C/450°F/Gas mark 8 for 15 minutes. Then reduce the heat to 180°C/350°F/Gas mark 4 and continue cooking for a further 20 minutes.

Cooking time: 35 minutes.

SAGO AND APPLE MOULD

	Metric	Imperial	American
Fine sago	100 g	4 oz	1 cup
Water	900 ml	1½ pt	3¾ cups
Apples	450 g	1 lb	1 lb
Sugar	100 g	4 oz	½ cup

Place the sago and water in a saucepan. Soak overnight. Next day bring to the boil and simmer gently until the grain clears. Peel, core and slice the apples and stew them until soft. Add the sugar and continue cooking to form a stiff pulp. Remove from the heat. Stir into the sago and mix thoroughly. Pour into a wet mould. When chilled, turn out and serve.

Cooking time: 30 minutes.

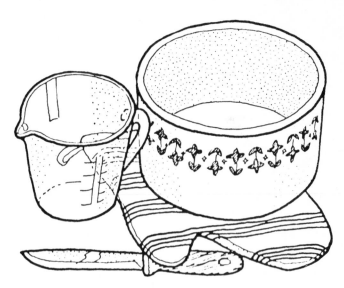

BROWN RICE PUDDING

	Metric	Imperial	American
Short grain brown rice	50 g	2 oz	¼ cup
Muscovado sugar	50 g	2 oz	¼ cup
Pinch of salt			
Super creamy milk-free milk (page 146)	600 ml	1 pt	2½ cups
Tomor	15 g	½ oz	1 tbsp
A little grated nutmeg			

Wash the rice and place in a greased oven-proof dish. Sprinkle with the sugar and salt. Pour on the milk. Dot with Tomor and sprinkle with grated nutmeg. Bake at 140°C/275°F/Gas mark 1 for 2½–3 hours.

Cooking time: 2½–3 hours.

APRICOT CRUNCH

	Metric	Imperial	American
Dried apricots	340 g	12 oz	¾ lb
Cold water			
Self-raising flour	100 g	4 oz	1 cup
Tomor	50 g	2 oz ·	¼ cup
Natural demerara sugar	50 g	2 oz	¼ cup

Cover the apricots with cold water and leave overnight. Next day, drain them and place in an oven-proof dish. Put the flour in a mixing bowl. Rub in the Tomor until the mixture resembles fine breadcrumbs. Add the sugar. Mix thoroughly and spread evenly over the fruit. Bake at 180°C/350°F/Gas mark 4 for about 30 minutes.

Cooking time: 30 minutes.

SWISS PUDDING

	Metric	Imperial	American
Tomor	25 g	1 oz	2 tbsp
Apples	450 g	1 lb	1 lb
Muscovado sugar	75 g	3 oz	⅓ cup
Water	2 tbsp	2 tbsp	2 tbsp
Fresh grated suet	75 g	3 oz	1 cup
Breadcrumbs (white or wholemeal)	175 g	6 oz	1½ cups

Heat the oven. Grease a pie dish with Tomor. Peel, core and slice the apples. Put them into a saucepan. Add the sugar and water. Cook gently to a pulp. Mix the suet with the breadcrumbs. Place alternate layers of the breadcrumb mixture and apple purée in the prepared pie dish. Finish with a layer of the breadcrumb mixture. Dot with Tomor. Bake at 220°C/425°F/Gas mark 7 for about 30 minutes.

Cooking time: 30 minutes.

BUTTERSCOTCH TART

	Metric	Imperial	American
Rich eggless shortcrust pastry (page 135)	175 g	6 oz	6 oz
Super creamy milk-free milk (page 146)	150 ml	¼ pt	⅔ cup
Cornflour	25 g	1 oz	⅓ cup
Water	2 tbsp	2 tbsp	2 tbsp
Made coffee	1 tsp	1 tsp	1 tsp
Demerara sugar	75 g	3 oz	⅓ cup
Tomor	1 tsp	1 tsp	1 tsp
Vanilla essence	1 tsp	1 tsp	1 tsp

Line a 18 cm/7 inch flan ring with the pastry. Bake blind at 190°C/375°F/Gas mark 5 for about 25 minutes. Remove from the oven and allow to cool. Boil the milk in a saucepan. Blend the cornflour with the water and add to the boiling milk. Cook for 5–7 minutes. Remove from the heat. Add the remaining ingredients. Reheat, mixing thoroughly. Allow to cool. Pour into the flan case. Chill.

Cooking time: 30–40 minutes.

GINGERBREAD PUDDING

	Metric	Imperial	American
Plain flour	350 g	12 oz	3 cups
Baking powder	1 tsp	1 tsp	1 tsp
Salt	½ tsp	½ tsp	½ tsp
Ground ginger	1 tsp	1 tsp	1 tsp
Fresh grated suet	100 g	4 oz	1 cup
Molasses sugar	25 g	1 oz	4 tbsp
Golden syrup	225 g	8 oz	1 cup
Super creamy milk-free milk (page 146)	scant 300 ml	scant ½ pt	scant 1¼ cups

Well grease a pudding basin with Tomor. Sieve the flour, baking powder, salt and ginger into a mixing bowl. Add the suet and sugar. Warm the syrup in a saucepan over a low heat. Add the milk and mix together until they combine. Remove from the heat. Stir into the dry ingredients. Mix well and turn into the prepared basin. Cover with greaseproof paper and steam for about 3 hours.

Cooking time: 3 hours.

SUMMER TARTS

	Metric	Imperial	American
For the tart cases:			
Rich eggless shortcrust pastry (page 135)	225 g	8 oz	8 oz
For the filling:			
Canned or fresh fruit e.g. strawberries, raspberries, cherries, peach slices, mandarin oranges			
Redcurrant jelly	6 tbsp	6 tbsp	6 tbsp
Water	1 tbsp	1 tbsp	1 tbsp
For the decoration:			
Milk-free whipped cream (page 150)	150 ml	¼ pt	⅔ cup

Heat the oven. Roll out the pastry. Cut into rounds with a scone cutter. Grease 12 tart tins with Tomor and line with the pastry. Prick the base and bake blind at 190°C/375°F/Gas mark 5 for about 10 minutes. Allow to cool in the tins. When cool, arrange the fruit in the tart cases. Melt the jelly with the water over a low heat. Cool slightly, then spoon over the fruit. Leave until the glaze is cold. Pipe round the edge of each fruit tart with milk-free whipped cream.

Cooking time: 10 minutes.

FESTIVE MINCE PIES

	Metric	Imperial	American
Milk-free shortcrust pastry (page 133)	225 g	8 oz	8 oz
Mincemeat	450 g	1 lb	2 cups
For the decoration:			
Icing sugar	175 g	6 oz	1⅓ cups
Warm water	1–2 tbsp	1–2 tbsp	1–2 tbsp
A few drops green colouring			

Roll out the pastry. Cut into 24 rounds with a scone cutter. Grease the tart tins with Tomor and line with the pastry. Place a teaspoonful of mincemeat in each tart case. Bake at 220°C/425°F/Gas mark 7 for 15 minutes. Remove from the oven. Leave to cool.

To make the white glacé icing, sieve the icing sugar into a bowl and add the water a drop at a time until the icing is thick enough to coat the back of a spoon. Spread three-quarters of the icing evenly over the cooled mince tarts. Add a few drops of green colour to the remaining icing and pipe the outline of a Christmas tree onto each tart. Leave to set.

Cooking time: 15 minutes.

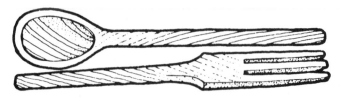

SUMMER PUDDING

	Metric	Imperial	American
Stale bread, 6 mm/¼ in thick	5 slices	5 slices	5 slices
Prepared fresh fruit e.g. raspberries, redcurrants, stoned cherries	450 g	1 lb	1 lb
Caster sugar	100 g	4 oz	½ cup
Water	225 ml	8 fl oz	1 cup

Remove the crust from the bread. Cut 4 slices into fingers. Reserve one slice for the top. Line a pudding basin with bread fingers. Put the fruit, sugar and water into a saucepan. Cover and cook slowly for about 10–15 minutes. Remove from the heat and fill the bread-lined basin with the stewed fruit and syrup. Place the remaining slice of bread on top. Cover with a plate or saucer. Press it down firmly. Put a weight on top and leave in the refrigerator overnight. Turn out.

Serve with chilled Milk-free whipped cream (page 150).

Cooking time: 15 minutes.

CHOCOLATE AND HONEY ICE-CREAM

	Metric	Imperial	American
Water	3 tbsp	3 tbsp	3 tbsp
Powdered gelatine	1 tbsp	1 tbsp	1 tbsp
Super creamy milk-free milk (page 146)	900 ml	1½ pt	3¾ cups
Vanilla essence	2 tsp	2 tsp	2 tsp
Clear honey	4–5 tbsp	4–5 tbsp	4–5 tbsp
Light muscovado sugar	50 g	2 oz	¼ cup
Drinking chocolate	5 tbsp	5 tbsp	5 tbsp

Put the water into a small basin. Add the gelatine and dissolve over a pan of hot water. Leave to cool. Warm the milk in a saucepan. Add the vanilla essence, honey and sugar. Mix well. Stir in the dissolved gelatine. Pour into a shallow freezer tray. Cover and freeze for about 3 hours until not quite hard. Next put half the frozen mixture into the liquidiser. Blend until smooth. Then pour into a chilled mixing bowl. Repeat the process with the remaining half. Stir the drinking chocolate into the creamed mixture and mix until well combined. Return to the freezer tray and freeze for a further 2 hours.

Freezing time: 5 hours.

Variation: To make **Fruit and honey ice-cream**, make as above replacing the drinking chocolate with 300 g/11 oz/1½ cups fresh, washed and hulled strawberries or raspberries.

BREAD AND PASTRY

WHITE BREAD

	Metric	Imperial	American
Fresh yeast	15 g	1/2 oz	2 tbsp
Sugar	1/2 tsp	1/2 tsp	1/2 tsp
Lukewarm water	just over 500 ml	just over 3/4 pt	just over 2 1/4 cups
Melted lard or white vegetable fat	1 tbsp	1 tbsp	1 tbsp
Plain white flour	800 g	1 3/4 lb	1 3/4 lb
Salt	1/2 tbsp	1/2 tbsp	1/2 tbsp

Put the yeast into a warmed mixing bowl. Sprinkle on the sugar and cream together. Add the water, lard and about one-third of the flour, sifted with the salt. Beat until smooth. Next beat in the remaining flour. Turn out onto a board and knead well. Place in a large greased mixing bowl, cover and leave in a warm place until double in size. When risen, knead again. Divide into 3 portions and place in 3 greased 450 g/1 lb loaf tins. Leave to rise again until double in size. Heat the oven. Place a large shallow tin of boiling water in the bottom of the oven and leave in during baking. Do not add more water. Place the risen dough in the oven and bake at 240°C/475°F/Gas mark 9 for 10 minutes. Then reduce the heat to 200°C/400°F/Gas mark 6 and continue baking for a further 30–35 minutes.

Cooking time: 40–45 minutes.

WHOLEMEAL BREAD

	Metric	Imperial	American
Fresh yeast	15 g	½ oz	2 tbsp
Sugar	½ tsp	½ tsp	½ tsp
Lukewarm water	600 ml	1 pt	2½ cups
Melted lard or white vegetable fat	1 tbsp	1 tbsp	1 tbsp
100% wholemeal flour	800 g	1¾ lb	1¾ lb
Salt	½ tbsp	½ tbsp	½ tbsp

Follow the method for White bread in the previous recipe.

MILK-FREE SHORTCRUST PASTRY

	Metric	Imperial	American
Plain flour	225 g	8 oz	2 cups
Salt	½ tsp	½ tsp	½ tsp
Tomor	50 g	2 oz	¼ cup
White vegetable fat or lard	50 g	2 oz	¼ cup
Cold water	2 tbsp	2 tbsp	2 tbsp

Place flour and salt in a mixing bowl. Rub in the Tomor and white fat until the mixture resembles fine breadcrumbs. Mix to a firm dough with the water. Knead lightly until the bowl is clean.

MILK-FREE WHOLEMEAL PASTRY

	Metric	Imperial	American
100% wholemeal flour	225 g	8 oz	2 cups
Salt	½ tsp	½ tsp	½ tsp
Tomor	75 g	3 oz	⅓ cup
White vegetable fat or lard	50 g	2 oz	1⅓ cup
Cold water	3 tbsp	3 tbsp	3 tbsp

Place the flour and salt in a mixing bowl. Rub in the Tomor and white fat until the mixture resembles fine breadcrumbs. Mix to a firm dough with the water. Knead lightly until the bowl is clean.

SWEET MILK-FREE SHORTCRUST PASTRY

	Metric	Imperial	American
Plain flour	225 g	8 oz	2 cups
Salt	½ tsp	½ tsp	½ tsp
Caster sugar	1 tsp	1 tsp	1 tsp
Tomor	50 g	2 oz	¼ cup
White vegetable fat or lard	50 g	2 oz	¼ cup
Cold water	2 tbsp	2 tbsp	2 tbsp

Put the flour, salt and sugar into a mixing bowl. Rub in the Tomor and white fat until the mixture resembles fine breadcrumbs. Mix to a firm dough with the water. Knead lightly until the bowl is clean.

RICH EGGLESS SHORTCRUST PASTRY

	Metric	Imperial	American
Plain flour	225 g	8 oz	2 cups
Caster sugar	25 g	1 oz	4 tbsp
Ground almonds	25 g	1 oz	¼ cup
Tomor	150 g	5 oz	⅔ cup
Water	2 tbsp	2 tbsp	2 tbsp

Put the flour, sugar and ground almonds into a mixing bowl. Rub in the Tomor until the mixture resembles fine breadcrumbs. Mix to a firm dough with the water. Knead well until the bowl is clean.

SUET PASTRY

	Metric	Imperial	American
Plain flour	225 g	8 oz	2 cups
Salt	½ tsp	½ tsp	½ tsp
Suet	100 g	4 oz	½ cup
Cold water	2 tbsp	2 tbsp	2 tbsp

Place the flour and salt in a mixing bowl. Mix in the suet. Mix to a firm dough with the water. Knead lightly until the bowl is clean.

BASIC REFRIGERATED CRUMB CRUST

	Metric	Imperial	American
Digestive biscuits (page 107)	175 g	6 oz	6 oz
Tomor	75 g	3 oz	⅓ cup
Molasses sugar	50 g	2 oz	¼ cup

Place the biscuits in a polythene bag and crush with a rolling pin. Melt the Tomor in a saucepan. Remove from the heat. Add the sugar and crushed biscuits. Mix well. Press the mixture firmly over the bottom and sides of a Tomor greased flan tin. Chill until set.

GINGER CRUMB CRUST

	Metric	Imperial	American
Traditional ginger nuts (page 106)	175 g	6 oz	6 oz
Tomor	75 g	3 oz	⅓ cup

Make as Basic refrigerated crumb crust, above.

SAUCES AND DRESSINGS

MILK-FREE SAVOURY WHITE SAUCE

	Metric	Imperial	American
Flour	2 tbsp	2 tbsp	2 tbsp
Super creamy milk-free milk (page 146)	150 ml	¼ pt	⅔ cup
Water	150 ml	¼ pt	⅔ cups
Salt and pepper			

Put the flour into a saucepan over a low heat. Pour in a little of the milk and blend to a smooth paste. Then add the remaining milk and water and season to taste. Stir continuously until the sauce thickens.

Cooking time: 5 minutes.

Variations: Make the sauce as above. When cooked, add the chosen ingredients.
For **Herb sauce**, add 2 teaspoons of mixed dried herbs.
For **Parsley sauce**, add 1–2 tablespoons of finely chopped parsley.
For **Creamy onion sauce**, add 1 finely chopped cooked onion.
For **Shrimp sauce**, add ½ teaspoon of anchovy essence and a few shrimps.

TOMATO SAUCE

	Metric	Imperial	American
Onion, chopped	1 small	1 small	1 small
Garlic, chopped	1 clove	1 clove	1 clove
Tomor	15 g	½ oz	1 tbsp
Tomatoes, chopped	225 g	8 oz	½ lb
Stock or water	150 ml	¼ pt	⅝ cup
Salt and pepper			

Gently simmer the onion and garlic in the Tomor. When translucent, add the tomatoes and stock. Cover and simmer for 5–10 minutes. Rub through a sieve and add seasoning to taste.

Cooking time: 10 minutes.

Variation: Tomato juice or paste can be used instead of fresh tomatoes.

BREAD SAUCE

	Metric	Imperial	American
Super creamy milk-free milk (page 146)	150 ml	¼ pt	⅔ cup
Water	150 ml	¼ pt	⅔ cup
Onion	1	1	1
Clove	1	1	1
Fresh breadcrumbs (white or wholemeal)	½ cup	½ cup	½ cup
Salt and pepper			
Pinch of cayenne pepper			

Put the milk, water, onion and clove in a sauce-pan. Bring to the boil. Add the breadcrumbs. Season with salt, pepper and cayenne. Simmer gently for about 15 minutes. Remove from the heat and take out the onion and clove. Mix well.

Cooking time: 15 minutes.

BROWN SAUCE

	Metric	Imperial	American
Onions	2	2	2
Carrots	2	2	2
Tomor	50 g	2 oz	¼ cup
Flour, white or wholemeal	40 g	1½ oz	⅜ cup
Stock	600 ml	1 pt	2½ cups
Salt			
Pepper			
Tomato purée	1 tsp	1 tsp	1 tsp

Peel and chop the vegetables. Heat the Tomor and fry the onions and carrots. Stir in the flour and continue cooking until the flour is light brown. Remove from heat and gradually stir in the stock. Return to the heat and simmer gently for about 30 minutes. Strain and season with salt, pepper and tomato purée.

Cooking time: 30 minutes.

HORSERADISH SAUCE

	Metric	Imperial	American
Milk-free savoury white sauce (page 137)	300 ml	½ pt	1¼ cups
Horseradish, finely grated	3 tbsp	3 tbsp	3 tbsp
White vinegar	1 dessert-spoon	1 dessert-spoon	1 dessert-spoon
Pinch of caster or light muscovado sugar			

Beat all the other ingredients into the milk-free white sauce. Serve with roast beef or trout.

BARBECUE SAUCE

	Metric	Imperial	American
Onion	1	1	1
Tomato ketchup	4 tbsp	4 tbsp	4 tbsp
Vinegar	2 tbsp	2 tbsp	2 tbsp
Crushed garlic	1 clove	1 clove	1 clove
Dry mustard	1 tsp	1 tsp	1 tsp
Lemon juice	1 tbsp	1 tbsp	1 tbsp
Molasses sugar	2 tbsp	2 tbsp	2 tbsp
Worcester sauce	1 tbsp	1 tbsp	1 tbsp

Peel and grate the onion. Mix all the ingredients well together.

Brush on steaks, chicken portions, chops or hamburgers while cooking.

RASPBERRY SAUCE

	Metric	Imperial	American
Raspberry seedless jam	2 tbsp	2 tbsp	2 tbsp
Juice of ½ lemon			
Caster sugar	2 tbsp	2 tbsp	2 tbsp
Water	150 ml	¼ pt	⅔ cup

Place all the ingredients in a saucepan and boil for 10 minutes.

Cooking time: 10 minutes.

Variations: Any flavour of seedless jam can be used to make different sweet fruit sauces such as **Apricot sauce** with apricot jam, **Strawberry sauce** with strawberry jam, and so on.

Note: Lemon curd and lemon cheese contain eggs.

MILK-FREE SWEET WHITE SAUCE

	Metric	Imperial	American
Cornflour	1 tbsp	1 tbsp	2 tbsp
Custard powder	½ tsp	½ tsp	½ tsp
Super creamy milk-free milk (page 146)	300 ml	½ pt	1¼ cups
Light muscovado or caster sugar	2 tbsp	2 tbsp	2 tbsp
Vanilla essence	½ tsp	½ tsp	½ tsp

Put the cornflour and custard powder into a saucepan over a low heat. Pour in a little of the milk. Blend to a smooth paste. Add the remaining milk. Stir continuously until the sauce thickens. Add the sugar and vanilla essence. Simmer gently for about 2 minutes, stirring continuously.

Cooking time: 5 minutes.

MILK-FREE CREAMY CUSTARD

	Metric	Imperial	American
Custard powder	2 tbsp	2 tbsp	2 tbsp
Caster sugar	1–2 tbsp	1–2 tbsp	1–2 tbsp
Super creamy milk-free milk (page 146)	600 ml	1 pt	2½ cups

Put the custard powder in a basin. Add the sugar. Mix smoothly with a little Super creamy milk-free milk. Put the rest of the milk on to heat. When nearly boiling, pour onto the mixed custard. Stir well. Return the custard to the pan and bring to the boil, stirring continuously.

Serve on egg-free, milk-free puddings and pies.

ORANGE SAUCE

	Metric	Imperial	American
Cornflour	1 tbsp	1 tbsp	1 tbsp
Custard powder	¼ tsp	¼ tsp	¼ tsp
Super creamy milk-free milk (page 146)	300 ml	½ pt	1¼ cups
Light muscovado or caster sugar	2 tbsp	2 tbsp	2 tbsp
Finely grated rind and juice of 1 orange			

Put the cornflour and custard powder into a saucepan over a low heat. Pour in a little of the milk. Blend to a smooth paste. Add the remaining milk. Stir continuously until the sauce thickens. Add the sugar and orange juice and rind. Simmer gently for about 2 minutes, stirring continuously.

Cooking time: 5 minutes.

CHOCOLATE SAUCE

	Metric	Imperial	American
Terry's Bitter Bar (or Home-made milk-free chocolate, **page 155)**	50 g	2 oz	½ cup
Knob of Tomor			
Super creamy milk-free milk **(page 146)**	1 tbsp	1 tbsp	1 tbsp

Melt the chocolate and Tomor in a small basin over a pan of hot water. Add the super creamy milk-free milk. Stir well. Serve at once.

Note: See page 9 on the use of cocoa and coconut products.

MILKS, DRINKS AND CREAMS

Do not give Basic soya milk or Super creamy milk-free milk to babies under weaning age.

BASIC SOYA MILK

	Metric	Imperial	American
Soya flour	100 g	4 oz	1 cup
Cold water	1.1 litre	2 pt	5 cups
A few drops vanilla essence			

Put the soya flour and water into a large saucepan. Bring slowly to the boil, stirring constantly. Add a few drops of vanilla essence to flavour and simmer gently for about 20 minutes. Remove from the heat. Rest a sieve over the top of a wide heat-resistant jug. Put a fine cloth inside the sieve, making sure the cloth overlaps. Strain the soya milk. Keep in the refrigerator. Stir well before use.

Cooking time: 20 minutes.

SUPER CREAMY MILK-FREE MILK

	Metric	Imperial	American
Basic soya milk (page 145)	150 ml	¼ pt	⅔ cup
Water	300 ml	½ pt	1¼ cups
Tomor or recommended milk-free margarine	25 g	1 oz	2 tbsp

Place all the ingredients in a saucepan. Heat gently until the Tomor has melted. Remove from the heat. Pour into a liquidiser and blend until the liquid turns creamy white. It usually takes about 1 minute. Keep covered in the refrigerator.

Use as ordinary milk in recipes that need milk, on milk-free breakfast cereals, in drinks, or by itself, well chilled.

CREAMY HOT CHOCOLATE

	Metric	Imperial	American
Super creamy milk-free milk (page 146), hot	1 mug	1 mug	1 mug
Drinking chocolate	2 heaped tsp	2 heaped tsp	2 heaped tsp

Place in the liquidiser. Blend until frothy. Sweeten to taste. Serve immediately.

CREAMY COFFEE

	Metric	Imperial	American
Super creamy milk-free milk (page 146), hot	1 mug	1 mug	1 mug
Instant coffee powder	1½ tsp	1½ tsp	1½ tsp

Place in the liquidiser. Blend until frothy. Sweeten to taste. Serve immediately.

MILK-EGG-FREE MALTED MILK

	Metric	Imperial	American
Super creamy milk-free milk (page 146), hot	1 mug	1 mug	1 mug
Malt extract BP	1 tbsp	1 tbsp	1 tbsp

Place in the liquidiser. Blend until frothy.

LEMONADE

	Metric	Imperial	American
Lemon	1	1	1
Sugar	2 tbsp	2 tbsp	2 tbsp
Cold water	750 ml	1¼ pt	3¼ cups

Place in the liquidiser. Blend well. Strain before serving.

BANANA AND HONEY SHAKE

	Metric	Imperial	American
Banana	*1 small*	*1 small*	*1 small*
Honey	*2 tsp*	*2 tsp*	*2 tsp*
Super creamy milk-free milk (page 146), chilled	*300 ml*	*½ pt*	*1¼ cups*

Place in the liquidiser. Blend until frothy.

CHOCOLATE SHAKE

	Metric	Imperial	American
Super creamy milk-free milk (page 146), chilled	*300 ml*	*½ pt*	*1¼ cups*
Drinking chocolate	*2 tsp*	*2 tsp*	*2 tsp*
Sweeten to taste			

Place in the liquidiser. Blend until frothy.

BLACKCURRANT SHAKE

	Metric	Imperial	American
Super creamy milk-free milk (page 146), chilled	300 ml	½ pt	1¼ cups
Blackcurrant juice	1 tbsp	1 tbsp	1 tbsp

Place in the liquidiser. Blend until frothy.

TOMOR BUTTER CREAM

	Metric	Imperial	American
Tomor	100 g	4 oz	½ cup
Icing sugar	225 g	8 oz	1¾ cups
Super creamy milk-free milk (page 146)	1–2 tbsp	1–2 tbsp	1–2 tbsp
Vanilla essence			

Cream the Tomor and sugar together. Gradually beat in the super creamy milk-free milk and a few drops of vanilla essence until the mixture is smooth and creamy.

Variations: For **Chocolate butter cream**, omit the vanilla essence and 1 tablespoon of Super creamy milk and add 25 g/1 oz of melted Terry's Bitter Bar or Home-made chocolate (page 155).

FRUIT SHAKES

	Metric	Imperial	American
Super creamy milk-free milk (page 146), chilled	300 ml	½ pt	1¼ cups
Fresh fruit, e.g. strawberries, apricots or raspberries	2 tbsp	2 tbsp	2 tbsp
Sugar to taste			

Place in the liquidiser. Blend until frothy. Strain before serving.

MILK-FREE WHIPPED CREAM

	Metric	Imperial	American
Tomor	100 g	4 oz	½ cup
Caster sugar	2 heaped tbsp	2 heaped tbsp	2 heaped tbsp
Hot water	2 tbsp	2 tbsp	2 tbsp
Super creamy milk-free milk (page 146), chilled	2 tbsp	2 tbsp	2 tbsp

Cream the Tomor and sugar until light and fluffy. Whisk in 1 tablespoonful of hot water, then 1 tablespoonful of super creamy milk-free milk. Whisk well. Add the remaining water and milk and whisk until thick. This takes a few minutes. Chill. Use as a topping for desserts or cakes.

BUTTERS, ICING, CHOCOLATE AND CAROB

Herb butters. Herb butters may be used to enhance the flavour of soups, grilled steaks, hamburgers, fish, jacket potatoes and many more dishes.

For a tasty sandwich, spread the herb butter of your choice on white or wholemeal bread before filling with meat or poultry.

Storing flavoured butters. Flavoured butters may be stored in the freezer for a period up to three months, with the exception of garlic butter, which may be stored for one month only.

CHIVE BUTTER

	Metric	Imperial	American
Tomor	100 g	4 oz	½ cup
Chopped chives	2 heaped tsp	2 heaped tsp	2 heaped tsp
Salt and pepper			

Slightly soften the Tomor. Add the chives, season with salt and pepper. Cream together until evenly blended. Shape into a roll and chill. Cut into slices as required.

Serve on fish, poultry or jacket potatoes.

Variation: For **Mint butter**, use chopped mint instead of chives.

MARJORAM AND THYME BUTTER

	Metric	Imperial	American
Tomor	100 g	4 oz	½ cup
Thyme	1 heaped tsp	1 heaped tsp	1 heaped tsp
Marjoram	1 heaped tsp	1 heaped tsp	1 heaped tsp

Slightly soften the Tomor. Add the thyme and marjoram and cream together until evenly blended. Shape into a roll and chill. Cut into slices as required.

Serve with soups, vegetables, pork and beef.

PARSLEY BUTTER

	Metric	Imperial	American
Tomor	100 g	4 oz	½ cup
Fresh chopped parsley	4 heaped tsp	4 heaped tsp	4 heaped tsp
A twist of freshly ground black pepper			

Slightly soften the Tomor. Add the parsley and pepper and cream together until evenly blended. Shape into a roll and chill. Cut into slices as required.

Serve on meat, fish, poultry and vegetables.

ORANGE BUTTER

	Metric	Imperial	American
Tomor	100 g	4 oz	½ cup
Caster sugar	225 g	8 oz	1 cup
Fresh orange juice	1 sherry glass	1 sherry glass	1 sherry glass

Cream the Tomor and sugar together until light and creamy. Gradually add the orange juice and mix well. Pile the butter onto a serving dish and chill until firm.

Serve with hot steamed puddings.

EGGLESS FONDANT ICING

	Metric	Imperial	American
Water	150 ml	¼ pt	⅔ cup
Caster sugar	450 g	1 lb	2 cups
Pinch of cream of tartar			

Dissolve the sugar in the water over a low heat until it forms a syrup. Add the cream of tartar. Boil until the liquid reaches 115°C/240°F. Pour slowly into a heat-resistant bowl and leave until a skin forms on the surface. Stir vigorously with a wooden spoon until firm and knead until smooth. The icing can then be wrapped and kept in a cool place until needed. Before using, place in a bowl over hot water and stir thoroughly adding a little sugar water if necessary to make the icing the consistency of thick double cream.

GLACÉ ICING

	Metric	Imperial	American
Icing sugar	175 g	6 oz	1⅓ cups
Warm water	1–2 tbsp	1–2 tbsp	1–2 tbsp

Sieve the icing sugar into a bowl. Gradually mix in the water a drop at a time until the icing is thick enough to coat the back of a spoon.

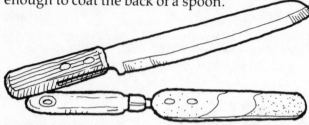

EGGLESS ALMOND PASTE

	Metric	Imperial	American
Icing sugar	100 g	4 oz	¾ cup
Caster sugar	100 g	4 oz	½ cup
Ground almonds	225 g	8 oz	2 cups
Lemon juice	1 tsp	1 tsp	1 tsp
Almond essence			
Bicarbonate of soda	½ tsp	½ tsp	½ tsp
Warm water	1 tsp	1 tbsp	1 tbsp

Sieve the icing sugar into a bowl. Add the caster sugar and ground almonds and mix well. Add the lemon juice and a few drops of almond essence. Dissolve the bicarbonate of soda in the water and gradually add to the bowl, stirring and then kneading to form a soft dough.

HOME-MADE MILK-FREE CHOCOLATE

	Metric	Imperial	American
Cocoa powder	12 tbsp	12 tbsp	12 tbsp
Softened white vegetable fat	4 tbsp	4 tbsp	4 tbsp

Place the cocoa and vegetable fat in a basin over a pan of hot water. Blend until smooth.

Note: This makes 100 g/4 oz of chocolate.

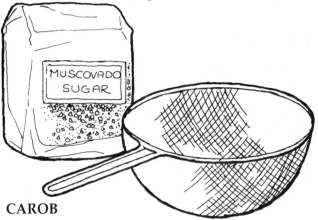

CAROB

Carob flour is obtained from the seeds of the locust bean, the fruit of the carob tree, a legume that grows in the Near East and the Mediterranean. For many years carob has been used by the food industry as a thickening agent, and as an alternative to chocolate. Some proprietary carob products contain milk. Use carob sparingly. Always store carob flour in an airtight container.

CAROB COATING

	Metric	Imperial	American
Tomor	50 g	2 oz	¼ cup
Icing sugar	8 heaped tbsp	8 heaped tbsp	8 heaped tbsp
Carob flour	3 heaped tsp	3 heaped tsp	3 heaped tsp
Super creamy milk-free milk (page 146)	2 tsp	2 tsp	2 tsp

Put the Tomor into a warm mixing bowl. Sieve in the icing sugar and carob flour. Cream together and beat in the milk.

CAROB ICING

	Metric	Imperial	American
Icing sugar	225 g	8 oz	1¾ cups
Carob flour	1 heaped tbsp	1 heaped tbsp	1 heaped tbsp
Warm water	2 tbsp	2 tbsp	2 tbsp

Sieve the icing sugar and carob flour into a mixing bowl. Add the warm water. Mix to a thick creamy consistency.

USEFUL ADDRESSES

GREAT BRITAIN AND EIRE
Allergy. Action Against Allergy,
43 The Downs, London,
SW20 8HG.
Midlands Asthma and Allergy Research Association,
12 Vernon Street, Derby, DE1 1FT.
National Society for Research into Allergy,
PO Box 45, Hinckley, Leicester, LE10 1JY.
Asthma. Asthma Research Council, St Thomas's
Hospital, Lambeth Palace Road, London, SE1 7EH.
The Chest, Heart and Stroke Association,
65 North Castle Street, Edinburgh.
The Chest, Heart and Stroke Association,
28 Bedford Street, Belfast.
Colitis, Crohn's Disease. NACC,
3 Thorpefield Close, Marshalwick,
St Albans, Herts.
Eczema. National Eczema Society,
Tavistock House North,
Tavistock Square, London, WC1H 9SR.
Mrs V. Brenthan,
5 Woodbine Road, Blackrock,
County Dublin.
Migraine. British Migraine Association,
178a High Road, Byfleet, Weybridge,
Surrey, KT14 7ED.
Migraine Trust,
45 Great Ormond Street, London WC1N 3HD.

AUSTRALIA
Asthma. Asthma Foundation of Tasmania, PO Box
18, Hobart, Tasmania 7001.
Eczema. Australasian College of Dermatologists,
271 Bridge Road, Glebe, Sydney, NSW 2037.

CANADA
Allergy. Allergy Information Association, Room 7,
25 Poynter Drive, Weston, Ontario.
Asthma. Asthma Information, c/o The Toronto Lung
Association,
157 Willowdale, Toronto, Ontario.
Eczema. Canadian Dermatological Association,
11 Cote Pedu Palais, Quebec City, Quebec, G1R 2J6.

USA
The Asthma and Allergy Foundation of America,
801 Second Avenue, New York, NY 10017.
The Society of Pediatric Dermatology, 4200E
Ninth Avenue, B-153, Denver, Colorado 80262.

INDEX

158